Nailing Jelly to the Wall:

Defining and Providing Technical Assistance in Early Childhood Education

by

Nancy P. Alexander

Also by Nancy P. Alexander:

Early Childhood Workshops That Work! The Essential Guide to Successful Training and Workshops

NAILING JELLY TO THE WALL

Defining and Providing Technical Assistance in Early Childhood Education

Nancy P. Alexander

Copyright

© 2012 Nancy P. Alexander

Published by Gryphon House, Inc.

PO Box 10, Lewisville, NC 27023

800.638.0928; 877.638.7576 (fax)

Visit us on the web at www.gryphonhouse.com.

Cover photography courtesy of iStock Photo, LP. All rights reserved. 2012. iStockphoto® and iStock® are trademarks of iStockphoto LP. www.istockphoto.com.

Interior photography courtesy of Shutterstock, LLC. www.shutterstock.com.

Library of Congress Cataloging-in-Publication Data

Alexander, Nancy P., 1941–

  Nailing jelly to the wall : defining and providing technical assistance in early childhood education / by Nancy P. Alexander.

   pages cm

  ISBN 978-0-87659-413-1

  1. Teachers' assistants--In-service training. 2. Early childhood education. I. Title.

LB2844.1.A8A53 2012

371.1—dc23

                    2012017532

ISBN: 978-0-87659-413-1

Bulk Purchase

Gryphon House books are available for special premiums and sales promotions as well as for fund-raising use. Special editions or book excerpts also can be created to specifications. For details, contact the director of marketing at Gryphon House.

Disclaimer

Gryphon House, Inc., cannot be held responsible for damage, mishap, or injury incurred during the use of or because of activities in this book. Appropriate and reasonable caution and adult supervision of children involved in activities, and corresponding to the age and capability of each child involved, is recommended at all times. Do not leave children unattended at any time. Observe safety and caution at all times.

Table of Contents

Introduction

What Is Technical Assistance?

Are you a coach, helping others in the early childhood field to improve their skills and knowledge? Are you a mentor, serving as a role model for those who are building a career in this profession? Are you a consultant, offering an objective, outside view of what is needed to improve a program or offering onsite help by providing resources, demonstrations, and guidance? Maybe you are a program administrator, working with your own staff to provide professional development and guidance.

Whatever you call yourself, what you have in common is that you are working to help other adults learn. You are all providing technical assistance, which is targeted, reflective professional development that offers advice, assistance, and training by a professional who understands both the subject matter and how adults learn. The goals of technical assistance are to develop learners' knowledge bases and to strengthen their application of best practices so they can be more effective teachers. Accomplishing these goals can be as challenging as nailing jelly to the wall.

This book is designed to help you go beyond simply talking about what needs to be done to improve a program or implement new procedures. The chapters in this book and the activities in each chapter are designed to assist professionals in providing the resources and guidance needed to scaffold each learner's development of the skills necessary for working with young children.

Who Are the People Who Provide Technical Assistance?

This book is written for professionals who are preparing onsite technical assistance sessions—professionals who have experience working with young children and who also have a background in the field of early childhood education.

The technical assistance sessions in this book include opportunities to provide examples from your own experiences, to incorporate comments and ideas from the learners with whom you are working, and to help these learners relate the content of the technical assistance sessions to their own work situations.

Characteristics and Roles of Technical Assistance Providers

The people who provide the best technical assistance are those who are knowledgeable and experienced and whose own enthusiasm for their work is so contagious that they inspire others just by doing what they enjoy most. However, the goal of technical assistance is to encourage the total growth of a (usually) less experienced person whose needs and interests are your primary consideration. What you do and how you do it will depend on who is receiving technical assistance, as well as that person's skills, background, and experience. Let's look at the important characteristics and roles of professionals who provide technical assistance:

Characteristics of a Professional Who Provides Technical Assistance

- Companion
  - Enjoys doing things with others
  - Shares interests and experiences with other adults
  - Spends time listening to and talking with others

- Supporter
  - Helps others to acquire knowledge, information, or skills
  - Boosts a learner's self-esteem and confidence
  - Conveys warmth and cares about the person receiving technical assistance
  - Supports the efforts of others
  - Listens to and responds to ideas and concerns
  - Expresses belief in the abilities of others

Roles of a Professional Who Provides Technical Assistance

- Role Model
  - Models and demonstrates appropriate ways of working with children, influencing the learner's behavior, values, and standards of practice
  - Conducts activities to demonstrate the skills and techniques being addressed
  - Provides a model for professionalism and appropriate behavior and attitudes
  - Is a person whom others admire or emulate
  - Has qualities, values, and skills that the learner desires
  - Expands the perspective and definition of what it means to work with young children

- Planner
  - Selects, designs, or plans the learning experience and the sequence of learning activities in collaboration with the learner
  - Responds with additional suggestions and follow-up activities
  - Adapts plans based on identified needs and interests

- Instructor
  - Plans and guides the learning situation—suggests but does not prescribe what a learner might do to solve a problem or improve a situation
  - Uses many open-ended questions to help the learner think through possible strategies and evaluate a course of action
  - Demonstrates to others how to perform tasks

- Facilitator
  - Helps the learner assess needs, set personal goals and timelines, and develop a plan of action to meet the goals
  - Responds to the learner's requests or interests; provides ongoing guidance and support as new behaviors, strategies, or procedures are implemented
  - Helps the learner to problem solve when steps do not go as planned and to evaluate progress in meeting goals

- Resource Person
  - Suggests books, supplies, and other sources of information based on the needs and goals of the learner and assists in determining appropriate uses that support the learner's plans
  - Provides guidance on accessing useful resources
  - Encourages the learner to approach others as resources and to make use of community resources
  - Shares ideas and suggests successful methods and strategies
  - Provides information to the learner in a helpful, considerate manner

- Co-Learner
  - Learns along with the learner, sharing ideas and experiences in a collaborative environment
  - Helps the learner recognize that there is rarely only one way to perform a task; the challenge is to find or develop the way that works best for the learner, the children in her class, and the program

- Confidence Builder
  - Encourages the learner to tackle new challenges and to engage in growth-enhancing experiences
  - Invokes confidence in skills and abilities and sets new goals through strategic activities that build on prior success

- Advocate
  - Assists in removing barriers to a learner's progress
  - Works to facilitate environments to maximize learning opportunities
  - Helps the learner understand how to suggest changes appropriately
  - Introduces the learner to new people, places, interests, and ideas

What Skills and Knowledge Does a Provider of Technical Assistance Need?

- Strong Interpersonal Skills
  - Enjoys working with other adults
  - Is patient; understands that change takes time
  - Is a good listener and reacts without judgment
  - Has the ability to initiate contacts and identify possibilities for improvement
  - Is able to help the learner feel successful
  - Is confident of her own abilities and knowledge
  - Is willing to share personal experience relevant to the needs of the learner

- Strong Supervisory Skills
  - Is able to help the learner set developmental goals, create action plans, and schedule deadlines
  - Is able to give feedback and coaching to reinforce positive behavior and progress
  - Is willing to assume and demonstrate leadership

- Knowledge of Resources and Opportunities
  - Knows where professional development and career opportunities exist and how to access them
  - Is familiar with state and department rules, policies, and procedures
  - Knows where and how to get help for many problems
  - Is a good problem solver and can lead the learner to discover resources to address needs and problems

- Interest in Someone Else's Growth
  - Would help another adult to learn through a supportive relationship
  - Can adapt and follow the learner's lead
  - Would allow the learner to develop at her own speed

Personal Reflections

Think about your early years in this field. Are there any individuals who were particularly influential? Who were some of these people who made a positive difference in your life? Use your answers to help you understand not only the value of providing technical assistance but also how to glimpse how learners may feel about you.

1. Why do you think the people you remember took a special interest in your success and desired to help you?
2. What qualities did you have that made them spend time with you and encourage you?
3. What were some things you learned from them?
4. What was it that made each of them a great mentor? What did these important people have in common?
5. What might these experiences teach you about how you want to be as a mentor to others?
6. How can you use this information in your own role as a mentor?

Why Technical Assistance?

Many learners want or need specific assistance in applying their skills in their work settings. By providing this assistance, onsite technical assistance plays an important role in program improvement. Technical assistance supports the implementation of change by providing:

1. Information or resources for program development.
2. An ongoing and supportive relationship between an experienced practitioner with a newer or less experienced person.
3. Defined goals and developed action plans that are an important means to ongoing professional development.

What do learners indicate that they want from technical assistance? Most want opportunities to:

1. Ask questions individually.
2. Receive answers to questions they have regarding their work.
3. Express their ideas in a supportive environment.
4. Find out about appropriate resources or referrals.
5. Complete assignments that result in progress.
6. Receive reassurance they are performing well.

What do learners indicate that they do *not* want from technical assistance? Most do *not* want someone:

1. Pushing them to make changes for which they are not ready.
2. Confusing them with too many ideas or too much information at one time.
3. Making them feel that they are doing things incorrectly.

What professionals providing technical assistance can do:

1. Provide a framework for solving problems.
2. Assist learners in setting their own goals.
3. Help learners identify and clarify the tasks they want to address.
4. Break tasks down into small steps.
5. Recognize and acknowledge effort and progress.

Principles for Productive Conversations

Productive conversations are essential to the success of technical assistance. Here are five principles to facilitate engaging and dynamic interactions:

1. **Be Aware:** Enhance your awareness of both the tangibles and intangibles in the program or in the group's interactions. Look past the obvious, and view any situation with an eye toward determining what's going on and the dynamics of the program. Seek information, and use that information, along with your own observations, to help determine what needs to improve and what skills to use to facilitate the change.
2. **Create Comfort:** Being clear about the process can create a comfortable environment in which the learner will communicate freely. Clearly describe what will occur and what is involved in the process. Explain the outcomes, clarify roles and processes, and help the learner provide input.
3. **Be a Mirror:** Help the learner become aware of her own process and her capabilities; focus the attention on the children and their needs, along with the learner's needs. Remember, she will most likely reflect to you the same levels of commitment and interest that you project.
4. **Stay Objective:** As a neutral party, you may become the recipient of complaints or frustrations. Remember that your role is to remain neutral and not to take sides.
5. **Focus on Outcomes:** Your role is to help the learner achieve her stated outcomes. Strengthen your facilitation skills and be prepared to focus on the outcomes—but allow for input and participation.

Communication and Problem-Solving Strategies

Listed below are a variety of communication and problem-solving strategies to consider when interacting with adult learners:

Helping Others Solve Problems: Think about a time you tried to help a friend with a problem. Did all attempts to help turn out perfectly? That is doubtful! Even when we come with the purest of intentions, many of our helping attempts seem to fail. Why?

Who Owns the Problem? When someone brings us a problem, we often have a tendency to try to give that person an answer that will solve her problem. We may ask a few questions, make an assessment, and offer a solution we feel will work, feeling as if we have been a good friend or coworker.

The problem with this approach is that we may not be the best at solving another's problem, or we are encouraging dependency on our expertise rather than the other person learning problem-solving skills. The person who has the problem is in the best position to solve the problem. Why? She is closest to the situation.

So why do others ask for help with solving a problem if they already know the answers? Sometimes, other people want to know that another person understands and is willing to listen without passing judgment. Sometimes, it is a matter of wanting confirmation that the solution they have selected is viewed as correct by another person whom they respect.

Communication Roadblocks: When you are providing technical assistance and trying to help others, your interactions may revolve around asking questions, giving advice, and offering reassurance and similar responses. Although these are appropriate tools, they can become communication roadblocks if used in the wrong situation. You might use a shovel to dig dirt out of a hole, but it would be the wrong tool for a delicate archeological dig. Likewise, when another person has a problem, we need to lose the roadblocks and use the right tools so the other person develops her own problem-solving skills.

Listening for Understanding: Most of us know that to express our interest when we listen to others, we make eye contact, nod, and say things like, "Uh huh," "Really?" and "Wow!" This is an important first step in listening, but it will not entirely help a person learn to solve her own problem. In order to help another person, we must listen for understanding.

An effective communication tool to use is active listening, a method of repeating your understanding of what the other person is saying and feeling. Eliminating communication roadblocks along with active listening helps others feel understood. The result? A higher success rate in problem solving.

Factors in Working with Adults

Adult learners are goal driven; they often participate in professional development with a purpose in mind. They usually want to improve their skills in specific areas where they either need help or see a benefit to themselves. Their goal may be to do their jobs better or to get a better job, or they may seek professional development because they want help with a specific child or a child-care problem, or because they want to interact effectively with their workers or coworkers. Adults want technical assistance that uses materials that reflect real-life situations and challenges, and they need to see how the activities will advance their goals. In addition, most adults learn best if the knowledge, skills, and strategies they are expected to acquire are linked to situations similar to their own or illustrate ones that they regularly encounter or that they feel they likely will encounter.

Adult Learners Need Opportunities to:

- Explore and discuss what they already know, what they would like to learn, how they are progressing in learning new skills, what barriers they encounter, and how they can overcome those barriers.
- Identify short-term and long-term goals, both general and specific.
- Assess their current knowledge and skills and evaluate and mark their own progress.
- Process new information by talking about ideas and discussing them with others.
- Work with others to learn collaboratively and become a resource for their own learning.
- See how others handle the challenges they encounter.
- Observe someone more experienced handle tasks similar to those they cope with daily.
- Be both challenged and supported as they try to upgrade their skills and acquire new strategies.
- Receive constructive and supportive feedback on their performance with suggestions for ongoing progress.

Adult Learning Principles

- Adults like to determine their own learning experiences.
- They enjoy small-group interactions and learn from the experiences of others as well as their own.
- Adults are motivated to learn when they identify they have a need to learn.
- They dislike having their time wasted.

- Adults draw their knowledge from years of experience and may not wish to change readily.
- They want practical answers for today's problems and practical problem solving.
- Physical comfort promotes learning.
- Learning takes place informally and through planned educational sequences.
- Recognition of similarities and differences between past experiences and present situations facilitates the transfer of learning.
- Learning "how to learn" enables adult learners to cope with the expansion of knowledge and changes in society.

Learning is:

- An active and continuous process manifested by growth and changes in behavior.
- More useful when it becomes generalized into principles and concepts.
- More effective when there is immediate application of what is being learned.
- Facilitated by proceeding from the simple to the complex and from the known to the unknown.
- Facilitated when the learner has the opportunity to test ideas, analyze mistakes, take risks, and be creative.
- Influenced by the learner's perception of herself and the situation in which she finds herself.
- Facilitated when the material to be learned has relevance to the learner.
- Dependent upon the readiness, emotional state, abilities, and potential of the learner.
- More effective in situations in which satisfaction is derived.

Changes in behavior and practices rarely happen overnight. Learning takes time, and regular review and reinforcement are vital parts of the learning process. The activities in this book are designed to be used with a learner one-on-one to make the activities relevant to her work setting. However, the activities can also be used to review the content of a training session or by a director or administrator to improve the skills of her staff. Also, many activities may be used as part of a staff meeting or as a basis for assessing needs and planning additional training.

Follow-up and onsite assistance make technical assistance sessions successful. Adults need reinforcement and review for new skills to become a habit and to feel totally comfortable in their new capabilities. Adults often need help in relating new information they have learned to their unique situations and working environments.

Technical Assistance: It's about Change

Various forces motivate the behavior of change agents, and when you provide technical assistance, you are a change agent. When someone tries new practices, it is often because she is motivated to find better ways to do things. This motivation may be external, based on circumstances outside the person's control, such as a new job requirement, or internal, from a desire to improve or achieve a skill, such as learning a specific computer skill to communicate with family members.

Stages of Change

The following section outlines some of the steps in the progression of change to help you understand what is involved and to help you guide the progress of change.

Process of Change:

1. Recognizes the need for change
2. Seeks a better way to do things
3. Determines what should be changed and how
4. Forms a tentative plan for the proposed change
5. Predicts probable reactions for the change
6. Forms a timeline or deadline for making the change
7. Implements the change

The learner, however, may embrace change, resist change, or have a mixed reaction. Prepare for a range of reactions that may include accepting and adapting to change, responding to change with anger and resistance, becoming committed to the new environment, or resisting any change.

Here are some initial questions that will help you as you work with learners to implement changes in programs:

- What would you like to improve in your program?
- Who are the people who will support the change?
- What resources do you need to make the change?
- How can everyone who is involved have input into the change?

Recognize that change is hard for many for a variety of reasons; learners facing changes may react in negative ways. The following chart comparing false hope and facts will help you understand the dynamics of change and prepare for negative reactions to change.

Feelings about Change

False Hopes	The Truths
Let's ignore it, and it will go away or be forgotten.	Change is here to stay. It is inevitable.
It will help if I get angry or upset about this.	Controlling emotions helps to increase control over the situation.
This is not good for my career.	Progress often requires change.
I can just keep on doing my job like I have been.	Expectations in the field are changing; you need to keep up, too.
Problems are encountered that prove that the changes won't work.	Problems are a natural side effect of the change process as new systems are implemented.
I can't make any difference, so what's the use?	You are either part of the solution or you are part of the problem.
They don't know what they're doing.	Even with a pretty good plan, change will involve running into problems or making some mistakes.
The changes weren't really necessary.	What's necessary now is to make the changes work.
The parents don't like the change.	The parents often see the benefits of the changes.
I just don't have the time for anything new.	Making new skills become a habit does take time and effort.
They're just going to lead us on and then drop the ax.	Failing to be open to new ideas and recognize change may mean there is no place for you.

Getting Started

Planning for the First Meeting

Before you undertake anything that is new, it is helpful to dedicate time to planning. Planning is a way to be clear about what you hope to accomplish and then to lay out some logical steps to help get you there. The following background information walks you through some steps to plan a first meeting. Create a companion version for the learner; you may want to send this to her before your first meeting so you will both be prepared.

Background Information

I will be providing technical assistance to: _____

Her phone number(s) _____

Her e-mail address _____

What would I like her to call me? _____

Has she been told who I am and that I will be calling?   _____ Yes   _____ No   _____ Don't know

Has she requested my help for a specific purpose?   _____ Yes   _____ No   _____ Don't know

If the answer is "no" or "don't know" and you are working through a formal program, contact the program staff and find out the status of this step. Calling before the learner has heard about you can make the first conversation awkward and confusing.

Ten Steps toward Intentionality in Technical Assistance

1. Find out about the learner and what she needs ahead of time.
2. Involve administrators as appropriate.
3. Be clear on what is to be accomplished.
4. Communicate with the learner and identify her responsibilities before, during, and after training.
5. Create a learner-focused plan for implementing changes.
6. Select learning activities based on objectives, jobs, tasks, interests, and needs.
7. Consider variety in activities and materials to address various learning styles.
8. Plan for follow-up and ongoing support.
9. Create templates or forms to use to document progress.
10. Recognize and celebrate improvement, progress, and achievement.

General Technical Assistance Guidelines

Preparing for Each Visit

1. Before the first meeting, talk with the learner and her administrator as part of your needs assessment to learn what each wants or needs the learner to address.
2. Review with the learner and administrator what you will do on the visit. Make it clear that you will be present as a helper and not an inspector.
3. Provide a means for the learner to contact you before each visit to ask questions and share her needs and concerns.
4. Be prepared. Review files and information. Refer to what was done in a prior visit.
5. Have a purpose in mind, but be flexible and adaptable to meet the learner's needs.
6. Be on time to scheduled visits, and be sensitive to the convenience of the visit.
7. State the purpose of your visit when you arrive if the visit is unscheduled.
8. Schedule ample time for feedback on the learner's progress. Remember that feedback must be specific, not just "good job."
9. Be familiar with community resources to make helpful and appropriate referrals.
10. Select examples and demonstrations that are familiar to the learner and relevant to her work situation.
11. Vary the instructional technique to address the specific learning style of the learner.
12. Keep the time agenda flexible to allow for important or off-topic discussions.

Behaving Professionally

1. Dress appropriately for the expected tasks.
2. Follow through on whatever you promise or agree to do.
3. Leave negative moods or feelings in your car. Maintain optimism for improvement.
4. Treat the provider and all others as professionals.
5. Avoid commenting on personal items.
6. Discuss only positive issues if guests or parents are present.
7. Remember that change is sometimes difficult and doesn't happen quickly.
8. Assist in correcting problems as soon as possible.
9. Summarize the visit, review the plans for the next visit, and thank the learner as you leave.

Building a Relationship

1. Spend time to get to know the learner and build rapport. Show respect and let her know you recognize the value of her work and want to help her in ways that will make her job more satisfying and fulfilling.
2. Build trust with the learner so she is comfortable asking questions.
3. Follow through on respecting confidentiality, and let her know that you will do so.
4. Pay attention to seating arrangements to promote interaction rather than an authoritarian style. Sit in a chair without a barrier, such as a desk or table, between you.
5. Understand that some learners will be nervous or uncomfortable.
6. Stay calm if you see something inappropriate. Take time to plan how to address the issue.

Meeting the Learner's Needs

1. Provide choices in what and how the learner may master or demonstrate mastery of the material.
2. Offer alternatives and choices in strategies and procedures to meet identified goals.
3. Demonstrate what you mean to avoid misunderstandings.
4. Explain the intent of a requirement or suggestion to help the learner understand why.
5. Integrate the new knowledge with what the learner already knows. Build on her strengths.
6. Allow for practice of new knowledge and skills in a supportive environment.
7. Support post-instruction performance with guides, checklists, charts, posters, and other tangible forms that document progress.
8. Minimize disruption to the learner's work and schedule. Emphasize that children's needs come first, and respect the learner's need to attend to children.
9. Use many open-ended questions to encourage communication.
10. Use language that is simple, direct, and understandable.
11. Offer suggestions in a constructive manner.
12. Use effective listening skills, and give the learner a chance to talk.
13. Make suggestions in small steps. Allow time for information to be absorbed.
14. Be specific when making plans. The learner needs to know exactly what is intended.

Tips for Success in Providing Technical Assistance

1. Use an outcome-based approach for planning: In developing your agenda for a technical assistance session, think about what will be different or what will happen by the end of the session. Write that outcome at the top of your plan to keep your focus. Ensure that all the activities work toward achieving that outcome.

2. Ask and record what has been working well so far. Mark and document progress while continuing to move toward the goal.
3. Use a visible "Who-does-what-by-when" action plan. Record commitments throughout the session and review and summarize the commitments at the end. Be sure the action plan is in writing, and use it to check progress at the next session.

Thinking Through the First Meeting

Typically, first meetings allow two people to get to know a little bit about each other, attach a face to a name, and become comfortable with the relationship. Select a setting that will feel comfortable for the learner and for you, and plan conversation starters.

First Impressions

What you do and do not do before and at the beginning of the first meeting will affect your success and rapport. Consequently, it is important to establish a professional atmosphere at the very beginning. Here's how to make a good first impression:

- Plan with clear objectives and meaningful activities.
- Practice giving instructions if you need to do so.
- Dress a bit more formally than you normally might if you lean toward casual attire.
- Arrive at the agreed-upon time.
- Set a friendly tone. Greet the learner by name.
- If you plan on observing in the learner's classroom, explain that you may be taking notes to help you remember things you want to discuss or questions you have.
- Make the learner feel comfortable with you as a person, but remain professional.
- Make productive use of the entire session. Keep focused on the task at hand. Treat time as a precious commodity.

Building Rapport

1. Introduce yourself. Learners are interested in knowing your background and experience. Your introduction reinforces your credibility as a professional. Provide information on your professional experience as a vehicle to make the material more relevant.
2. Get to know the learner. Find out why she is interested in receiving technical assistance and what she hopes to gain from it. Ask about her short-term and long-term goals for her career.
3. Ask open-ended questions. The more information you gather to build rapport, the more likely it is that the participant will trust you and be responsive. Ask her about her views, the problems she experiences, or reservations she has. Find things that you have in common and talk about them.
4. Use silence. When you ask a question, pause to let the person answer. Pausing shows the person that you really want to hear what she has to say. Use effective listening skills to hear what she is saying.
5. Be enthusiastic. Focusing on the learner will build rapport. Your interest will make her feel important and will generate trust. This will make her more receptive to your messages.
6. Be understanding. Let the learner know that you understand what her job is like and what challenges she has. When you acknowledge or demonstrate that you understand, it doesn't have to mean that you agree; it just means you have listened and comprehended. Make statements that demonstrate your understanding of her situation and needs.

Developing a Written Agreement

Consider working with the learner to develop a written agreement to clarify roles. A written agreement creates a commitment and dedication to the process, making it a priority for each person. Here is a sample to help you get started:

By creating and signing this agreement we, _____ and
_____, are committing to do our best to honor these rules.

As we spend time together, we will both try to:

- Meet at least once per _____, for at least _____ (amount of time).
- Pick meeting places that allow us to really talk.
- Give the other person at least 24 hours' notice if we have to cancel or reschedule a meeting.
- Come to our sessions prepared, having completed any assignments or gathered any resources per our previous discussions.
- Maintain confidentiality and respect privacy.
- Work on our common goals, which include the following:
  - (list goals here):

Making Learning Last

If you want the technical assistance you provide to truly impact the job environment, plan connected activities to do before, during, and after the technical assistance activities to help make the learning stick.

Before the activities:

1. Create a learner- and job-focused training plan.
2. Design the activities with specific job objectives, job tasks, and prerequisites in mind.
3. Include a variety of learning tools and techniques.
4. Make quick-reference cards for appropriate tasks.
5. Create a form to use to track progress.
6. Be sure that the decision-makers whose approval is needed support the change.

During the activities:

1. Incorporate on-the-job examples and supervised practice.
2. Motivate the learner throughout.
3. Vary approaches to presenting material and information.
4. Share your own examples.
5. Use commitment statements.

After the activities:

1. Use e-mail to follow up and send surveys.
2. Check that the learner is applying the skills.
3. Conduct follow-up interviews with administrators.
4. Use e-mail, text messages, and newsletter articles.
5. Determine areas that need additional attention.

Examples of Challenging Technical Assistance Scenarios

Below are some scenarios that you might encounter. Consider developing appropriate responses as you prepare for what you might encounter as you provide technical assistance.

1. A director has asked you to help Sandra improve her communication with parents. You observe Sandra at pickup time and note that her usual interactions with parents are to answer their questions simply, with one or two words. A mother asks about her child's eating that day and Sandra just answers, "She was fine," providing no additional information.

2. Maxine has asked for help with discipline. When you arrive, you see that the room is poorly arranged, with no clear traffic patterns or protected areas. You observe a number of conflicts among the children due to the lack of clearly defined interest areas and overall lack of organization.

3. Jacobi tells you he has some children who are very difficult to handle. When you visit, you note that most of the activities are geared toward children much older than the preschoolers with whom he works. You are aware that he started working in the program in the summer with school-agers and has recently started full-time with preschoolers.

4. You have developed good rapport with a new teacher who is showing much promise. Now that she feels comfortable with you, she begins to complain about the center where she is working. She asks you to be a reference for her to get another job. "This place is the pits!" she states. "The director thinks she's queen, and the other workers don't carry their loads." She also asks you not to tell the director she is planning to leave.

5. A center has had ongoing problems with illnesses among both children and staff. The director has asked for your help in providing training on sanitation. Following the training, Sophia, a head teacher, tells you it was a waste of time. "Nobody pays any attention to that stuff. Everybody knows about hand washing, but nobody does it."

6. You are observing in a classroom of three-year-olds when a child falls, scrapes his knee, and begins crying loudly. "I've got to take him to the office," the teacher tells you. "I'll be right back." You realize that the teacher aide is on break and you are the only adult in the room.

7. A center is required by the Bureau of Child Care Licensing to have technical assistance in playground supervision as a result of several recent accidents. Although adult ratios are adequate, teachers congregate and chat, thus not providing effective supervision. You held a staff meeting for them, explaining why they should not use the time for visiting. You discuss the importance of supervision. However, the situation has not improved even after several reminders.

General Technical Assistance Activities

The activities that follow can be used in most any situations to help evaluate needs, make a plan for improvement, and mark progress in implementation of new skills.

Action Plan for Learners: Help the learner make an action plan. Provide a blank copy of the **Action Plan** chart (see page 126) and help the learner create a plan to improve the area. On page 127 is a completed sample Action Plan for the Block Area that can be used as a guide.

If the learner is unable to assess what is not working, spend some time observing her and offer suggestions. Ask open-ended questions to ascertain if she has some ideas about what can be done to fix the problem. Support her own ideas about solutions, and be prepared to offer suggestions to expand on her efforts.

Inspector or Evaluator: Ask the learner to pretend that she is an inspector or an evaluator and must assess her own classroom. Tell her that just as a licensing inspector must see evidence of a regulation, she can only check off an item if she sees it. For example, if the checklist asks for a discipline policy to be posted, then she can check that item if she sees it posted, not just because she knows that the center has a discipline policy. Remind the learner to be very detailed and accurate in her evaluation. Then work with her as she checks off items on the list. The following is a brief sample of items that are in most licensing regulation. However, a checklist for this activity should be based on licensing regulations for individual states, on an evaluation tool used by the program for accreditation, or on state quality rating systems.

Sample Checklist for Licensing Regulations

- [ ] Electrical outlets are covered.
- [ ] Steps, stairways, hallways, and other walking areas are free of hazards.
- [ ] Menus are posted with any substitutions noted.
- [ ] Parents or other visitors sign in and out as required.
- [ ] An attendance record is kept on children as required.
- [ ] A schedule is posted and followed reasonably.
- [ ] The program's discipline policy is posted.
- [ ] Information about allergies is readily available to all staff.
- [ ] An emergency evacuation plan is posted.
- [ ] Fire drills are conducted regularly.
- [ ] A fire extinguisher is readily available, and all staff know how to use it.
- [ ] Outdoors is free of equipment hazards or any other hazard, such as broken glass.
- [ ] Children are dressed appropriately for the weather with extra clothing available.
- [ ] A written policy for handling and reporting accidents or incidents is available to all staff.

If criteria from licensing are used, this activity will help the learner be more aware of the regulations that she is required to follow. If a rating scale, such as the Early Childhood Environment Rating Scale, is used, then having her take on the role of evaluator can help her better understand quality and understand what she can do to improve her classroom's rating.

Schedule time to review her findings at the end of the activity. Then make a plan for improvement based on her inspection. The plan might be a simple list of tasks to be accomplished or an action plan.

ABC Activity: Ask the learner to research a topic and find one fact that goes with each letter of the alphabet. For example, if you were working on the topic of science activities, the results might begin like this:

A. Provide AMPLE materials.
B. Making BUTTER is a science activity children enjoy?
C. Support CURIOSITY.
D. Allow enough time for ideas to DEVELOP.
E. ENJOY science yourself.
F. Children enjoy FEEDING FISH.
G. GOLDFISH are relatively inexpensive.
H. Children can develop a HYPOTHESIS.
I. INCLUDE a variety of activities.

Providing Real-Life Scenarios: Presenting the learner with scenarios that are similar to what she has experienced is a good way to have the learner plan how to handle a situation she is likely to encounter. Write down situations that you recall from your own experiences to use in the process of providing technical assistance. The scenarios should require consideration of various courses of action. Use them as the basis for discussion of strategies, activities, and appropriate ways to react.

Development Activity: Discuss the domains of development—cognitive, language, physical, and social/emotional—with the learner. Ask her to find three ways to address each area of development based on what topic is being addressed. For example, if you are focusing on dramatic play, you might address the concept of cause and effect when using the materials, the language interactions in the home living area, the opportunities to move around and develop eye-hand coordination, and the chance to form friendships.

Internet Search: An Internet search for specific information not only helps the learner find the information but also helps her develop better computer skills and become familiar with websites that can be used for further information on other topics. Most topics can be addressed with an Internet search. Be sure to help the learner understand how to determine if a website is credible and likely to have accurate information. Your role is to help her interpret and evaluate the information she finds.

Crossword Puzzles and Word Finds: There are websites that allow you to make crossword puzzles and word finds easily. Making these from definitions you want the learner to understand adds fun to the session. They also can be great to use as a review.

Evaluation

Evaluation is an important tool for improvement in any job. Receiving feedback on how you have performed can help you do a better job. One type of evaluation is a formative evaluation, designed to be completed partway into a project to assess progress and implement change during a project. The **Formative Evaluation Report** on page 128 is a sample to consider using.

Another type of evaluation involves collecting data on how the learner felt about the help you provided. On page 129 is a **Satisfaction Survey,** another sample to consider using.

Another important tool is a report of each visit. This report creates and maintains a record of what is being accomplished during the onsite visits. On page 130 is a sample (**Family Child Care Home Technical Assistance Report**) that you may use or adapt to your needs.

How to Use This Book

If you are new to providing technical assistance, it is easy to fall into a routine of mostly talking about what can be done to help the learner improve her work. While such conversations might lead to some improvement, the real challenge is in helping the adult think about what is needed and how to achieve the improvement by herself. Guidance in thinking about changes and how to accomplish them can be provided by another interested adult through such activities as the ones that are included in this book rather than just discussion.

The activities in the introduction and in each chapter are designed to provide suggestions for activities and inspiration for approaching learning situations with adults. Depending on the situation that you are addressing, you might select one or two activities to use with an individual learner according to her needs or interests. In other situations, you might select many of the activities to introduce and then reinforce a thorough understanding of a topic. The activities are not intended to be a cookbook of technical assistance "recipes" to follow exactly, but instead to present suggestions that you can use to focus on what the learner needs.

If you are new to the role of providing technical assistance, using the collection of activities in this book, which are based on common topics, will give you guidance and suggestions that will allow you to help other adults.

If you are someone who is experienced with providing technical assistance, use the information and activities as written or as a springboard to create other activities. In addition, the activities may offer a fresh approach to stimulate your interest in and motivation for professional development experiences.

Each chapter provides an easy-to-use source for working with an individual in a one-on-one situation or in a small group setting. The activities are structured to build on what the learner already knows and what her current working environment is like, to maximize the use of the resources available to the learner.

Each chapter begins with a summary of the concepts to be developed by the learning activities in that chapter. At the end of each chapter is a list of questions that can be made into an evaluation tool to determine the learner's progress or to plan for additional activities.

The activities might also be used in staff meetings or as a part of a staff member's individual improvement plan. A lead teacher can use activities to provide information and support for a newly hired staff member. The activities might also be used for small group activities in a college class that has some members are more experienced than others. Additionally, the activities would be useful to a supervising teacher with an intern or student teacher.

In whatever way the book is used, there are some common strategies that will usually benefit the adult learners. Here are some suggestions:

Avoid overload. Too much content or too many tasks at once can overwhelm and frustrate the learner. Even in settings where extensive help is needed, it is important to tackle a few improvements at a time. Typically, spacing activities over time with regular reinforcement through communication will be more effective than trying to do many things all at once.

Allow time for practice. Spacing visits gives the learner time to work on the new skills and implement and become comfortable with new techniques. Regular visits and assistance over a few months supports the learner and scaffolds his improvement.

Identify and schedule the next step. Learners are usually anxious to either show what they have accomplished or to receive feedback on how they are doing. Scheduling the next visit gives a structure to the progress as well as a deadline that can keep learners working on the changes. A clear plan summarized at the end of a session is helpful to the learner in understanding exactly what she is going to do.

Remember key points. At the end of a technical assistance session, ask the learner to make a commitment to remember key points about the new information she has learned. Ask her to write the key points on an index card and to keep the index card handy for reference in the upcoming week. Point out how reading this information several times a day will help her remember to put it into practice.

Handouts and Worksheets

Throughout this book, the term *handouts* is used to identify materials that are usually one or two pages. These handouts are designed to be distributed to participants, read, and discussed. Worksheets are similar to handouts, but are intended for the participants to add to the content, usually by writing additional information on them. Many of the forms in this book as designed to be used as worksheets.

Boldface Titles

The specific names of forms, charts, and handouts are written in boldface type when referenced in each chapter. All forms are at the end of this book; however, the page number of each form will be included in the text.

Chapter 1 Technical Assistance:
Room Arrangement

Room Arrangement: Why Does It Matter?

What Is the Indoor Environment?

Discuss the indoor environment with the learner. Help her to understand that although the focus is often on the room arrangement, the indoor environment also includes:

- All materials and activities inside the physical building.
- Everything that affects the child that occurs indoors.

Discuss how the indoor environment plays a vital role in young children's learning. For the environment to enhance children's learning, it must first be safe and healthy. However, the focus of the technical assistance you provide will be on the equipment, materials, and supplies that go into the classrooms and the arrangement of the items in a way that best facilitates learning and interaction.

Emphasize that for young children the environment *is* the curriculum. The equipment, materials, and supplies in the classroom; the arrangement of the furniture; and the interactions with the other children and the adults in the classroom should support the children's physical, emotional, social, and cognitive development. Therefore, it is critical to pay careful attention to what is in the classroom environment and how it is arranged.

You will explore the following together:

- The effect the environment has on children's learning and behavior.
- How to use classroom space and materials to create an interesting, secure environment that encourages play, exploration, and learning.
- How room arrangement affects the way children behave.

Number of Children versus Classroom Size and Interest Areas

Discuss how the number of children affects the size of the interest areas and the amount of materials in each area. The following are challenges related to the number of children and the classroom size:

> **Note**
>
> Interest areas are also called *learning centers* and *interest centers*. In this book, these terms will be used interchangeably.

- Negative and idle behaviors increase in situations with a high density of children and few resources or equipment.
- The quantity of resources should increase if there are many children using the interest areas.

Advantages to Learning Centers

Discuss with the learner how she thinks learning centers help children learn. Brainstorm the advantages of learning centers and why they are common to early care and education programs. Use the handout **Advantages to Learning Centers** on page 131 to talk about any advantages that were not included in the discussion. Ask the learner to share her experiences with learning centers, including what works well now and what areas have problems or need improvement.

Review or explain the typical learning centers including in most classrooms. Even small classrooms with limited equipment can have learning centers. Emphasize that such groupings help children learn to see relationships. Having learning centers reduces waiting time for children, a common behavior challenge.

Planning and Improving the Physical Environment

Evaluating the Classroom

To begin assessing what needs to improve in the indoor environment, discuss the learner's needs by asking her the following questions:

- Where are most of the discipline problems inside the classroom?
- What areas of the classroom are not used by the children?
- What is your most frustrating clean-up problem indoors?
- What have you tried to make or do to address these issues?
- What are your equipment or supply needs?
- What recycled or inexpensive items have you tried? How were they received?

Give the learner the list of questions that follow. Work with her to evaluate the existing learning centers in her classroom. Make a list of any problems that are identified and develop a plan to address those problems.

- Are the centers arranged with clear traffic patterns and boundaries?
- Are soft elements, such as rugs, pillows, and beanbags, included in each center?

- Is there a place in the room where children can be alone or with a few friends?
- Are there clear indications where things belong, such as pictures, labels, color coding, or paper shapes?
- Is there natural light and good artificial lighting, so the room is bright even on dark, dreary days?
- Does the noise level indicate busy, involved children?
- Is the room relatively free of clutter and unused materials?
- Are toys, equipment, and furniture cleaned regularly?
- Are all areas of development supported?

Targeting the Problems

Once the areas needing improvement are identified, use the chart **Indoor Environment Evaluation Log: Furnishings** on page 132 to determine changes that need to be made. Once the specific needs are identified, make an action plan (see page 28 in the Introduction) to determine how to proceed.

Room Arrangement Checklist

Once you and the learner identify an interest center that needs improvement, use the relevant section of the **Room Arrangement Checklist** on page 133 to see where changes need to be made. Add other factors to the list to address the specific needs of the learner or her classroom.

Establishing Interest Areas

If the learner is not currently using interest areas or is not using some of the suggested interest areas, use the following information about establishing interest areas to help her plan to set up the appropriate interest areas in her classroom. Help her assess which interest areas to address first.

Explain the following guidelines for establishing and arranging interest areas:

- Separate noisy areas from quiet ones. (For example, the blocks and home living centers should be located together; the library area and table toys should be located on another side of the room.)
- Clearly separate each area using shelves and furniture or other dividers.
- Display materials at a height accessible to children so they can see what choices are available.
- Separate children's materials from teachers' supplies.
- Logically place interest areas near needed resources (for example, the art area near water).
- Ensure that teachers can see all the areas without obstruction. Avoid hidden areas that limit supervision.
- Incorporate a traffic pattern that keeps children from constantly interrupting each other.
- Allow children to learn through exploration and active involvement with the materials.
- Provide a variety of materials and offer several choices for children.
- Display materials in an organized manner; label for selection and cleanup. Labels should include both printed words and a picture, shape, color, or outline of the materials.
- Change the choices in each center as changes are made in curriculum themes, and according to the interests of the children and the unique needs of individual children.
- Display the name of each center and the learning objectives for the center to inform and assist parents and visitors and help them understand the organization and purpose of the center.
- Use storage cabinets and dividers no more than 4 feet in height, unless secured.
- Discourage running and sliding by positioning learning centers in a way that avoids long open areas.
- Use tables and shelves to break up straight pathways.
- Set up activities in the centers to engage children's interest.
- Carefully define the areas to encourage children to stay there and expand on activities.

Interest Area Checklist Posters

Help the learner create Interest Area Checklist Posters to use as guides for creating or improving interest areas. Have available poster board or large sheets of paper, assorted supply catalogs, markers, scissors, and glue. Ask her to create a learning center using pictures from the catalogs or her own drawings. She may also list possible items if unable to locate pictures or if she wants to include donated items or items to be purchased from other sources. Then, as she is able to secure the items needed, she can check them off as a way of documenting progress in equipping her interest areas.

Evaluating Interest Areas

Give the activity sheet **Evaluating Interest Centers** on page 135 to the learner, and ask her to review it. Ask her to evaluate the interest area she created and to use the information on this activity sheet as a guide to continue to improve her interest areas.

Comparing Room Arrangements

Show the learner photos of two or more room arrangements: one or more that has good arrangements, and one or more that has problems with the arrangements. The goal is to give the learner experience in using the room arrangement guidelines and in looking for ways to improve room arrangements, not necessarily to show her an "ideal" plan. Guide her as she considers the following ideas to evaluate the room arrangements in two photos (photo A and photo B):

- Identify the strengths of the room arrangement in the photo A. Then, identify the weaknesses.
- Look at room arrangement in photo B. What is different? In what way is this arrangement better? How might it not be as good as the room arrangement in photo A?
- Draw or graph a plan of your classroom as it is now.
- What can you change in your room to help with guidance issues?
- Draw your classroom, showing how you want to rearrange it.

A

B

Graphing the Room Arrangements

Work with the learner to draw the classroom to scale on graph paper. Use equipment shapes and move them around to explore various arrangements to see how major items, such as shelves and tables, will best fit. Graphs and equipment cutouts are available from many school supply stores and catalogs. Address such factors as the quiet, noisy, and buffer areas; traffic patterns; and the amount of room necessary for the desired number of children in making the plan.

Traffic Patterns: Observe the learner's class during interest-area time, paying special attention to the traffic patterns and how the children move from one area to the other. Make a floor plan of the room showing the most common traffic patterns that you have observed. Review this information with the learner. Work with her to address any problem areas that are created as a result of room arrangements that do not include clear traffic patterns.

Photo Ideas: Look at the photos you used for comparing room arrangements, and talk with the learner about the advantages and disadvantages of the room arrangement in each photo. Help her locate items to add to interest areas or to create a plan to obtain additional materials.

Photo Cards for Discussion: Take digital photos of several learning centers. Write scenarios under the photos including open-ended questions to stimulate discussion.

What to Put in the Environment

Review the items currently available in the learner's classroom. Remove items that are broken, incomplete, inappropriate for the ages of the children, in the wrong location, not used by the children, or otherwise best removed or replaced. Discuss with the learner the following information about selecting or purchasing materials and equipment. Review the information together, discuss it, and make a plan to address the items in question.

Criteria for Selecting or Purchasing Materials and Equipment

When evaluating whether to include material or a piece of equipment in your classroom, consider the following:

- Is the item safe and interesting for children of this age group?
- Does it keep the child involved?
- Is it developmentally appropriate?
- What area or areas of development does it support?
- Does it add balance to existing materials and equipment?
- Is it suitable for available classroom space?
- Is it durable? (Items that will not hold up to heavy use may be wasted money.)
- Does it complement the program?
- Does it require a minimum of supervision?
- Is it easy to maintain?
- Is there a sufficient quantity?
- Is it nonviolent?
- Is it multicultural?
- Is it nonsexist?
- Is it age appropriate? (Age designations do not fit all children; materials may be meant for some but not for all.)
- Is there an inexpensive substitute you can use?
- How can it be used for more than one purpose?
- How many children can use the items at a time?
- Does it balance the children's developmental needs? Is there an overall balance of items geared toward small-motor growth and gross-motor growth; quiet and noisy items; and individual and small-group items?

What Do I Need?

Work with the learner to make a list of items needed to improve her indoor environment using the ideas in **Suggestions to Build On**, which is on page 138. If many items are lacking, decide which items are a priority and develop a plan for the remaining items.

For Further Study

Ask the learner to research information about how the room arrangement affects the way children behave by searching one of the following topics on the Internet. Provide guidance in evaluating websites to select appropriate resources. Ask her to make copies of the information and to start a resource file for the material she locates. If needed, offer suggestions about how the learner can organize the material in either folders or notebook binders.

How Does Room Arrangement Affect the Way Children Behave?

- Using space to reduce discipline issues and promote positive interactions among children
- Using routines and scheduling to provide a predictable environment
- Helping children see relationships through the use of interest centers
- More ideas for how to use space and location effectively
- Teacher-made and inexpensive materials for learning centers
- The importance of aesthetics in the classroom and how to provide an aesthetically pleasing environment

Making It Work

Point out to the learner the importance of children having easy access to the materials but explain some guidelines for allowing access without chaos. Stress the importance of the total room arrangement and the relative location of interest areas—for example, noisy areas, such as the dramatic play area, should be away from quiet areas such as the library area. Consider the following:

- Involve the children in establishing limits, and remind the children of those limits.
- Model appropriate behavior in using, caring for, and cleaning up the material and supplies in the classroom.
- Provide ample toys and materials and meet the children's needs.
- Keep play areas uncluttered and organized; children and adults must be able to move freely without tripping or falling over materials.
- Remove broken toys or any with sharp, jagged edges or small parts.

Use some of the following ideas with the learner:

Before-and-After Scrapbook: To create a record of the progress of the technical assistance process, take a photo of the interest areas in the room before you begin working with the learner and again afterward. If she is interested, use the photos to create a scrapbook page on paper or using a digital scrapbook software program.

Posters for Communicating Children's Learning: Ask the learner to select an interest area and to make a poster about what the children learn in that area. Display the posters for parents and other staff to view.

Observing Traffic Patterns: Ask the learner to observe and track traffic patterns as the children use the interest areas. Identify where the children's movement creates disruptions, such as when children walk into the block area and knock down buildings. Using the information gathered, make a plan to relocate some items to create a better traffic flow.

Seeing the Child's Point of View: Help the learner to look at the room from the child's viewpoint. You will gain an entirely different view of the room when you get down on the floor and truly see it from the children's eye level. This activity is a good way to point out to the learner the importance of where to put displays and items intended for the children and to determine how the children see the room. Ask the learner what she learned from seeing the room from this point of view.

Evaluation of Technical Assistance

Use the following as a worksheet or questionnaire to assess the learner's mastery of technical assistance activities about room arrangement:

1. How does the arrangement of equipment, materials, and supplies affect what goes on in a classroom?
2. What are some reasons that using interest areas encourages learning?
3. Why is it important to consider traffic patterns, barriers, and locations of interest areas?
4. What are some guidelines for purchasing or selecting equipment?
5. Pick one interest area and suggest items to go in that area.
6. Describe factors to consider in setting up the interest area selected.

Chapter 2 Technical Assistance:
The Dramatic Play Area

Why Is Play Important?

What Does the Learner Know about the Value of Play?

Discuss with the learner her feelings related to play, and ask her to tell about a play activity she remembers from her childhood. Find out how she feels about play by asking her the following questions:

- What do you remember about play in your own childhood?
- What was your favorite game as a child and why?
- Can you remember anything you learned from those play activities?
- Did you and your friends ever play pretend and dress-up?
- What was the value to you of those play experiences?

Discuss what the learner gained through the games she played as a child. Use her examples to identify why play is important to young children. For example, she may remember examples of group play that involved cooperation, planning, and creativity. Help her to recognize the value of what she learned and how many important skills are developed through play. Point out how play can take place throughout the classroom and outdoors, but is especially supported through a specific dramatic play center. Describe how the focus of the technical assistance will be on the design, equipment, materials, supplies, and interactions that support play, including dramatic play, and thus will facilitate learning.

Explore the following together:

- How children's play supports their learning and how to communicate these benefits to families
- How to establish or improve the use of classroom space and materials to create an appealing and supportive area to encourage children's play, including dramatic play

- How to select and support the use of themes to provide a focus for children's play, to build on children's interests, and to expand on their existing knowledge
- How to interact with children during play to expand their concepts, problem-solving skills, and cognitive abilities to provide intentionality in learning

What Do We Mean by *Dramatic Play*?

Ask the learner to describe what she thinks of when she hears the words *dramatic play*. Work with her to develop her personal definition of dramatic play. Explain that there are many ways to define dramatic play, but that the following is what we will use:

Dramatic Play: Pretend play, or make-believe play, that involves taking on a role and engaging in imitative behavior.

The Benefits of Play

Brainstorm with the learner ideas about the benefits of play and the skills children develop through play. Explain that although the focus is on dramatic play, much of the information relates to other types of play as well. Use some of the concepts that follow to guide this activity.

- Play fosters a positive self-concept because the child is in control of what happens, and play is open-ended, meaning there are no right or wrong answers.
- Play stimulates problem solving as children figure out how to accomplish a task or goal.
- Play enables children to understand the world around them because they take on roles of others.
- Play allows children to express and resolve their feelings by acting out situations and experiences.
- Play enhances creativity because children use their imaginations to create play scenarios.
- Play develops social skills such as cooperation, compromising, negotiation, and making friends because most dramatic play involves others.
- Play encourages the use of materials and resources in creative ways as children find items to substitute for real items. For example, using a box for a baby bed, using a block for a pretend phone, or using construction paper to make money or debit cards.
- Play develops math and science skills through sorting, matching, ordering, planning, categorizing, measuring, counting, experimenting, and observing.
- Play develops auditory and visual perception skills and memory skills because children must remember their play scenarios.
- Play develops literacy and language skills because children must communicate their needs, thoughts, ideas, and observations.
- Play reduces stress as children act out their feelings and emotions.

Major Concepts about Play

Discuss with the learner the following major concepts about play. Ask her to tell you about some examples from her own experience. Help the learner to understand that these major concepts should be kept in mind when arranging for play experiences. Ask her to write these points on an index card to keep handy and to refer to during her day with children to remind her of these facts.

- Children learn from play.
- Adults can enrich play experiences.
- Props can stimulate play activities and learning.
- Open-ended questions help children to develop ideas.
- Play takes time and space.

Benefits of Open-Ended Play Activities

Observe the learner working with children who are engaged in dramatic play. After the observation, ask her for examples of why dramatic play is considered an open-ended activity. Discuss whether the children:

- Used their imaginations.
- Felt successful and in control.
- Enjoyed what they did.
- Presented no discipline problems.
- Worked according to their abilities and interests.
- Cleaned up willingly.

Benefits of Free or Dramatic Play

To relate the benefits of play to the developmental domains, review and discuss the handout **Benefits of Free or Dramatic Play** on page 140 with the learner. Give her a copy to keep handy for reference.

Evaluating and Improving the Dramatic Play Area

Assist the learner in evaluating her dramatic play area. Show her pictures from catalogs or photos that you have taken of good dramatic play arrangements. Provide a list of suggested equipment if needed to help her select appropriate purchases. Review the list with her, showing examples from various school supply catalogs. If purchases are not possible at this time, offer suggestions on what inexpensive substitutions or teacher-made materials might be used.

Setting Up a Dramatic Play Dress-Up Area

After assessing the dramatic play area, work with the learner to develop a plan for improvement. Initially, there likely will be a need for more or better materials. Use the handout **Setting Up a Dramatic Play Dress-Up Area** on page 142 and the action plan information in the Introduction to help her make a plan for improvement.

Setting Up a Dramatic Play Home Living Area on a Shoestring Budget

Although there is no good substitute for sturdy, well-made equipment, in some cases programs may be lacking funds and may need time to work a home living area into their budgets. Use the following information to guide the learner.

The home living area should be large enough for three or four children to use together. It is important to include a toy stove, refrigerator, sink, cupboard, and a table with chairs, as well as a doll bed with dolls, clothing, pillows, and blankets or sheets. Toy dishes, pots and pans, play food, and toy cleaning equipment will also stimulate play in this area. A toy iron, ironing board, and toy telephones add to the play ideas that children will have.

Sturdy boxes can be used to make a toy stove and sink. While they will not hold up nearly as well as wooden ones, they can be replaced free as needed and can help a teacher begin to provide home living play opportunities.

If a doll bed is not available, one can be made from a box. Pieces of fabric can be used for blankets. Check with parents to see if they will donate dolls their children no longer play with. If no small table is available, the end of a large table can be used for pretend meals.

Other possible accessories or props for the home living area are tablecloths and napkins, and a plastic vase and flowers to make a centerpiece. If dishes are needed, parents might donate some plastic ones they no longer use. Freezer containers, margarine bowls, or other containers can be used. Pots and pans which parents no longer use might be donated, too.

Photo Documentation

Take a photograph of the learner's dramatic play area before you begin working with her to improve a dramatic play center, and then take more photographs to document her progress in improving the area. Create a documentation poster or book to show the progression in improving the dramatic play area. The learner can use the documentation poster as a communication tool with parents or to report at a staff meeting how the area was improved.

Developing and Using Prop Boxes

Explain to the learner what prop boxes are and how they are used. Show some examples of prop boxes, and ask her what she thinks children could learn from each of the prop boxes.

Review the handout **Suggested Prop Boxes for Dramatic Play** on page 143 with the learner. Explain that a wide variety of items can be used for props. Show a sample prop box as an example of how to put one together. Point out that most of the materials in most boxes can be donated, so there is little or no expense involved.

Help her locate, evaluate, and organize items for several prop boxes, and assist her in organizing and planning for their introduction. Oversee and support the use of the prop boxes by asking her to try the items with the children for a few days and then meet with you to review and evaluate their success.

Ask the learner to copy the following headings onto a sheet of paper and to use the headings to develop a plan to create her own dramatic play theme prop box. Once she decides on a prop box topic, ask her to write the name of the prop box at the top of the paper.

When making a dramatic play prop box, consider the following:

- Purpose of this prop box
- Materials in this prop box
- Additional materials needed
- Preparation
- Activities for which the children can use the materials to role play
- Teacher support needed
- Where to get supplies

Assembling a Prop Box

Using the **Assembling Dramatic Play Prop Boxes** handout on page 145, discuss with the learner how she might assemble a prop box. Use the guidelines in the handout to structure the discussion. Ask her to select a topic for a prop box that she can put together for her dramatic play area and to use the approach described in the preceding paragraph to create a plan.

Parent Letter to Request Props

Help the learner develop a letter to request prop items from parents and other staff. Review safety and sanitation issues to address with used or recycled items. In a week or two, check with the learner to see what items have been received. Make suggestions on how the items might be used or other items that might be requested.

Selecting Appropriate Play Themes

Talk with the learner about using themes and why they are used. If she does not use themes for planning, introduce the concept of themes and explain why themes can be good planning tools. Help her understand that a theme provides a focus for the day or week. Introducing concepts in different ways reinforces what children learn by giving them opportunities to use new vocabulary, re-enact events, and learn the meaning of these concepts. Show the learner how providing fire hats for dress-up, adding fire trucks in the block area, completing puzzles about firefighters and trucks, singing songs about firefighters, and reading books about firefighters reinforce concepts that develop from a field trip visit to a fire station.

Discuss how using themes helps with planning because it provides the repetition and reinforcement that children need to learn concepts in various ways. Themes narrow choices to some degree, making it easier for the teacher to focus on selecting activities. Having a theme to plan around also helps prevent the teacher from getting into a rut by repeating the same popular activities too often.

Brainstorm with the learner topics for themes for various ages and list them. Give her some guidelines for selecting appropriate themes, and emphasize how to select themes according to children's interests. Point out how themes must be based on things with which the children are familiar. For example, outer space is not an appropriate theme, but pets, toys, or foods would be. Give additional examples of inappropriate themes, and use the following questions to guide the discussion of how to decide if a play theme is appropriate:

- Does the topic address children's interests?
- Is the topic age appropriate and relevant to the children's experiences?
- Can the children explore the topic firsthand though people to talk to, places to visit, or objects or living things to observe?
- Are enough resources available, such as books, songs, things to explore and observe?
- Can children apply a variety of skills in exploring the topic?

Decide on some possible themes that would be appropriate for the children with whom the learner works. After the learner selects several themes, ask her to evaluate each theme by using the following approach.

Selecting Appropriate Dramatic Play Themes

Answer the following questions related to the play theme selected.

- Why do you feel this theme will be appealing and interesting to the children?
- Is there a variety of roles for several participants? List some of the possible roles for children that might be included in the theme.
- Will the children have some basis in experience for the dramatic play situation? Describe what you might do to help children have experiences that will help them in the dramatic play roles that you listed previously.

Steps to Implement Play Themes

Use the following to help the learner plan how she is going to implement the play theme she has selected:

1. Decide what will be a whole-group, interest center, or individual activity.
2. Decide on a logical and reasonable timeline.
3. Gather materials and supplies for activities.
4. Set up and display the materials and supplies.
5. Introduce the theme and communicate expectations.
6. Evaluate as you go; adapt or change as necessary.
7. Make notes for future reference.
8. Communicate successes to parents and teachers.
9. Take advantage of the teachable moments to incorporate many skills.

Once the learner has successfully implemented a play theme, help her to select two to three themes to plan and implement in the near future.

Ways to Support Play

After observing how children function in the dramatic play area, discuss with the learner what she considers to be the adult's role in supporting play. Work with the learner to establish that the following guidelines can be followed to encourage and support play as needed.

- Provide ample space when setting up the dramatic play area.
- Arrange the area carefully.
- Allow uninterrupted blocks of time.
- Use props to suggest play ideas.
- Interact with children; ask many open-ended questions.
- Make cleaning up easy.
- Observe children's interactions to evaluate the activity for future planning.
- Expand the play by providing additional props or by taking a role in the play.
- Watch for possible conflicts and redirect the play if necessary.
- Enjoy play yourself.

Review the detailed information about how to support children's play to evaluate the learner's progress in creating a good environment for play. Work with the learner to decide together how well each criterion is met.

Creating an Environment for Play

Provide Space

- Arrange the dramatic play area carefully to reduce wandering and encourage social interaction.
- Limit the number of children allowed in the area to prevent overcrowding and related discipline problems.
- Provide indirect guidance to maintain order and simplify cleanup by:
  - Labeling shelves or containers with pictures or words.
  - Color-coding to facilitate organizing.
  - Selecting and storing accessories carefully.

Provide Time

- Encourage greater involvement with sizable blocks of time (at least 60 minutes).
- Consider how to support children's play with rainy-day schedules and at different times of the day, such as arrival and departure times.

Provide Materials

- Develop prop boxes.
- Vary interest centers.
- Relate play setups to current themes.

Enjoy Play Yourself!

- Support creative play with a good attitude.
- Interact with children in a way that shows you value their ideas.
- Follow the children's interests and ideas.
- Use open-ended questions to encourage ideas.

Summarizing How Teachers Can Support Dramatic Play

Discuss with the learner how she might help guide the play activities or address discipline issues by conducting nondirective interventions, such as taking part as a player. Use examples you have observed and the following guidelines to give her ideas for how that process can work.

1. Enter children's play as an observer, and comment or ask questions about what you see happening.
2. Provide props and materials based on the play activity to suggest more ideas.
3. Allow enough time for ideas to develop and for children to take on roles.

Talking to Children during Play

Many adults have difficulty in knowing how to interact with children during play. Use the following play interactions to help the learner learn to converse with children during play. Ask the learner to take the adult's role in each dialogue set and you take the child's role. Optionally, you might take the adult role in order to model what it could look like. There are two scenarios; each one includes one child and two adults with very different approaches. Use props as appropriate. Note that in some situations, it will be desirable to demonstrate incorrect responses to help the learner differentiate appropriate and inappropriate responses. After the scenarios are acted out, compare the responses from the adults in the two separate roles. Ask for observations and reflections about the responses from the learner, and ask her to suggest additional ways to respond to each situation.

Play Interactions

Scenario 1

Janie: You are Janie, a three-year-old with a new baby sister. Your mother lets you help with the baby, holding the bottle, getting diapers, and so on. Today, you want to use the doll in the home living area and show your friends how you and your mother care for your sister. You are in the housekeeping area with your friend.

Miss Dara: You are Miss Dara, a veteran teacher who has plans for children in the home living area to have a pretend grocery store today. You're determined that they will have experiences with fruits and vegetables to encourage good nutrition and to learn about buying and selling to develop math concepts. You see Janie and another child in the home living area playing with the doll, an activity not in your plans.

Miss Betsy: You are Miss Betsy, and you know that Janie has a new baby sister. You want to help her accept the new baby in the family and to feel good about her new role of big sister. You see Janie and a friend in the home living area.

Scenario 2

Paul: You are Paul, a four-year-old. You visited your father this weekend, and he gave you a large yellow truck that you brought to the center to show the other children and to play with. Your father has remarried and has moved out of town, so visits are infrequent. This truck is very important to you. You come beaming and happy into the classroom.

Ms. Mary: You are Mary, a new teacher who learned a rule in your student teaching setting: children may not bring items from home. You are inflexible and intend to enforce the rule. You confront Paul when he arrives.

Mrs. Jacob: You are Mrs. Jacob, and you have been working with four-year-olds for many years. You know about Paul's family situation and are aware of his need for understanding and support after a visit with his father. He especially feels displaced because his father now has stepchildren, one a boy only a year older than he is. You see Paul bringing the new truck into the classroom.

Selecting Books to Support Play

Assist the learner in selecting children's picture books from her own library or from the public library that include children involved in dramatic play activities. Discuss how these books might be used to stimulate play. Then, help the learner to review catalogs for possible book purchases that will be appropriate for stimulating dramatic play. Provide the learner with a list of suggested books appropriate for the age group with which she works, if needed.

Supporting or Hindering?

Point out some of the ways that adults can hinder play, using the following information to lead the discussion. Ask the learner to evaluate how effective she thinks that she is in avoiding the actions that hinder play with young children. If she feels she does act out some of these hindering behaviors, suggest that she list the ones she wants to change on an index card to remind her during the day.

Adults hinder play by:

- Correcting children's activities.
- Being too involved ("taking over").
- Redoing children's work (straightening towers, rearranging materials).
- Doing too much talking or directing.
- Encouraging competition by comparing.
- Over-teaching—too much emphasis on concepts and skills ("What color is that block?").
- Providing materials that are not age appropriate (either too difficult or not challenging enough).
- Cutting the time short—children need time to become involved and time for ideas to gel.
- Not allowing choices by assigning areas or roles.
- Providing too few materials or choices—or too many.

Adults support play by:

- Providing freedom within limits.
- Having a playful nature themselves.
- Accepting and enjoying children's play.
- Knowing when and how to introduce materials.
- Interacting appropriately by participating, not dominating, and by conversing, not interrogating.

Minimizing Challenging Behavior during Dramatic Play

When children interact in groups, there will occasionally be issues of behavior that must be addressed. Build on a situation you have observed and help the learner to see how some indirect methods can help her avoid or deal with the behaviors.

Typically when children are happily involved, discipline problems will be minimal, so the secret to avoiding or eliminating discipline problems is working to keep children involved and engaged. The following are a few ideas for minimizing challenging behaviors during dramatic play with young children:

1. To reinforce involvement and desirable interactions, try nondirective interventions, such as a smile or reassuring glance, a nonverbal message that it's okay to pretend and that you value what the children are doing and how they are involved in play.
2. Enter the play scene as an observer and comment or ask questions about what you see happening. This involvement makes the children more aware of what they are doing, and it will help redirect negative behaviors. Commenting on the activities or asking questions often stimulates more ideas for expanding the play activity. For example, asking children who are playing grocery store about what they intend to buy will get them thinking, planning, and talking, or it can redirect aggression toward focusing on a task.
3. Be an active participant; the teacher can take on a role and may demonstrate a particular skill such as how to make-believe with objects and situations. For example, with grocery store play, you might ask children if they can purchase certain items for you and discuss with them whether you want fresh, frozen, or canned items; how many items; or how to pick out the best bargain. As you participate, make sure that you avoid dominating the conversation. Be a participant, not a person in charge.

Ask the learner if anything about play makes her uncomfortable. If so, suggest she keep in mind that dramatic play allows children to work out difficult feelings and experiences. Ask the learner to suggest pretend play that might make her uneasy. If none are forthcoming, mention anger and aggression, and ask for an example she might have experienced. Discuss inappropriate role-playing behavior, such as acting out sex acts or pretending to use drugs and alcohol. Acting out feelings is one of the main purposes of dramatic play, but it is necessary to address what types of acting out are inappropriate. Within the context of a pretend role, you can redirect behavior; then, find a way to discuss rules about desirable behavior outside of the dramatic play episode. Avoid making judgments.

Putting It into Practice

Use the following questions to assess the learner's progress. These questions might be made into a questionnaire, a learning game, or a basis for producing a parent newsletter about play or preparing to make a staff meeting presentation about play.

1. Describe the importance of play.
2. Identify at least three appropriate play themes.
3. How and what skills do children learn through play?
4. Explain the role of adults in supporting and extending play.

5. What teacher skills or practices stimulate play?
6. What teacher behaviors restrict or hinder play?
7. Describe how to select appropriate themes for young children.
8. Discuss the ways that dramatic play enhances children's development.
9. Give some tips for selecting topics for prop boxes and prop box assembly.

Creating a Culture of Play

Parent Letter or Newsletter: As previously discussed, you can help the learner write a parent letter or a paragraph for a parent newsletter describing the value of play and the program's philosophy concerning play. Offer materials such as brochures or handouts to use as resources to develop the letter. Point out that this might be a good time to ask for materials.

Peer Assistance and Teamwork: Suggest that the learner team up with another staff member and observe each other's classrooms, focusing on how the children use the dramatic play area. After the observations, meet with both of them to share their suggestions and insight and to offer feedback.

Poster or Bulletin Board: Suggest that the learner make a poster for parents or a parent bulletin board to inform parents about what children learn through dramatic play. Offer materials to assist in creating the poster or bulletin board and resources for information about what to include. For example, a poster might include the following information:

Through dramatic play, children learn

- Cooperation and sharing,
- Language and reasoning skills,
- Problem solving and creative thinking, and
- Planning and following through on plans.

Employee Manual: If the program does not have a section on supporting play in its employee manual, help the learner write a section describing the program's approach to supporting play. If there is no employee manual, provide some samples to help the program begin to develop one, starting with some sample philosophy statements or mission statements about supporting play. If the program does have such statements, review and consider revising them.

Staff Meeting Plans: Help the learner plan for a staff meeting that will focus on dramatic play. Help in scheduling the meeting, planning the presentation, and finding or making resources. Suggest that some of the materials from the technical assistance you provided be used in the staff meeting.

Resource File: Help the learner gather and organize reference materials about dramatic play from books, journals, and magazines. Suggest a variety of ways to organize the materials, such as putting copies of handouts or journal articles in loose-leaf notebook binders or accordion folders. The following are a few topics to use to organize the resources in a notebook or accordion folder:

- The Value of Play
- Space Arrangement
- Ideas for Dramatic Play Themes

- Materials and Props
- Teacher Interaction and Support
- Parent Involvement Ideas

Computer Resources: In addition to the resource file of articles from books, journals, and magazines, ask the learner to search for reference materials on dramatic play on the Internet. Provide guidance in evaluating websites to select appropriate resources. Demonstrate how she can organize the material in computer folders and help to create folders for the websites selected. The folder titles listed above could be used to organize computer files or website favorites.

Dramatic Play Outdoors: Brainstorm with the learner what items might be used for dramatic play outdoors. Take a tour of the playground with her to evaluate and select a location to set up dramatic play. Make a list of ways that dramatic play might be supported with equipment, such as riding toys. See Chapter 5 on Technical Assistance for Outdoor Play for suggestions of books to read to children that might stimulate their ideas for dramatic play outdoors.

Evaluation of Technical Assistance

Use the questions below as a worksheet or questionnaire to assess the learner's mastery of the technical assistance activities about promoting play:

1. How do we teach concepts and cognitive skills intentionally through play?
2. What do you communicate to parents or administrators about play?
3. What can you do to encourage dramatic play outdoors?
4. What are suggestions for themes to encourage dramatic play?
5. How can you maximize space to keep children involved?
6. How do you explain the value of play to parents?
7. How can you prevent play from getting rough or out of hand?

Chapter 3 Technical Assistance:
The Library Area

The Value of Library Area and Reading to Children

Why Is a Library Area Important?

Discuss with the learner how a reading center may be referred to in various ways; it may also be called a *library area, book center,* or *literacy center.* Tell her that they all refer to the same thing, and these terms will be used interchangeably.

Then talk about the importance of a library area in the classroom. Discuss with the learner that the goal of this technical assistance is to help her support the literacy development of the children in her classroom and will include the following:

- How to equip and set up a library area or to improve on the one she has
- How to select appropriate books to meet the needs of various children and curriculum goals
- How to add writing opportunities to the classroom
- How to schedule additional time during the day for reading aloud to children or to allow them to enjoy books
- How to encourage families to enjoy books with their children

Use the following list to guide the discussion. A library area is a place for children to:

- Engage with other children in a less active interest center.
- Relax in a soft environment.
- Enjoy the world of literature.
- Be alone or with a few friends.
- Associate reading and books with relaxation and pleasure.
- See others reading and writing.
- Acquire a love for books, one of the most powerful incentives to become readers.

Ask the learner to describe a place where she relaxes and write down some of the key words describing her place to relax. Then ask her to circle or underline any of the words that could be included in the design of a library area.

Discuss the benefits of having a relaxing environment for reading. Show photos of library areas or use school supply catalogs for examples. Then ask the learner to reflect on her own arrangements for reading in the classroom and emphasize how the reading center is a place for children to get away from the busy activities of the classroom.

What Do Children Learn from Books?

Ask the learner what her favorite book was when she was a child, and have her discuss why she liked it and what she learned from it. Help her relate the importance of reading to children to language development and other literacy learning. Ask her about memories of being read to as a child and what was important about the experience.

Read *Brown Bear, Brown Bear, What Do You See?* or a similar book with the learner to demonstrate how children can learn concepts from having a book read to them. Discuss how exploring colors by reading a book and through other real-life experiences is an effective way for children to learn. Use the list below to discuss some other benefits of a having library center and of reading books to children. Depending on the book selected and the main character's experience, children can learn to:

- Expand their imaginations.
- Increase vocabulary and language skills.
- Appreciate the rhythm of language.
- Associate written words with meaning.
- Cope with difficult events, such as the following:
  - Divorce.
  - Death of a pet or family member.
  - Being hurt or hospitalized.
  - Natural disasters.
- Acquire knowledge of science, math, health, safety, history, and vocabulary.
- Learn social skills and responsibilities, such as the following:
  - Being a friend.
  - Sharing and taking turns.
  - Behaving in social situations.
  - Being a part of a family.
  - Being kind and cooperative.
  - Appreciating literacy.
  - Appreciating many cultures.
  - Understanding their feelings, fears, and questions.
- Develop motivation to read and write by:
  - Being read to regularly.
  - Being encouraged to look through books.
  - Listening to story tapes.
  - Making up their own stories.

Language and Literature: Meeting Children's Needs

Use the following information to help the learner understand the relationship between children's literature and children's developmental needs. Then, ask her to think about her classroom and how she uses books. Ask her to share with you examples of how language and literature help meet the following needs of young children.

Children need to know about their world: Children are curious about their world, and books can provide a way of learning information.

Children need to accept and to give love: Stories offer children a chance to meet characters who, like them, need love and affection.

Children need to belong: Literature can help children find other people who are like them.

Children need to achieve and to feel self-esteem: Children can find stories about characters who have succeeded against difficult odds, to help build self-confidence and a "If he can do it, so can I" attitude.

Children need beauty, order, and harmony: Children can find these characteristics in stories and illustrations and can apply them to their lives. The language in many books is beautiful in itself.

Children need to cope with stress and difficult events: Books help children cope with fears of darkness or monsters, pain, loss of a loved one or pet, separation or divorce, or natural disasters.

Setting Up a Library Area
What Do I Need to Set Up a Library Area?

Show the learner photos of some library areas, and discuss the pros and cons of each one. Review the following information with the learner. Help her evaluate what she has already that can be used to establish a library area if she does not have one. Brainstorm items that she might purchase or move from another area to establish a library area. Help her select items from a school supply catalog if she wants to purchase items.

How to Set Up a Library Area

- Include soft items, such as rugs, pillows, and furniture.
- Add plants for a pleasant, homelike environment.
- Display story-related puppets, puzzles, and story character toys.
- Have a flannel board at a child's height with an assortment of flannel board figures nearby.
- Display books with covers showing so children can easily select what they want.
- Have a core selection of favorite books available, but add new ones frequently, especially those you have read aloud.
- Label the center and post the number of children who can use it at one time.
- Find a location that will be out of the line of traffic and away from noisy areas such as the block or dramatic play areas.

To get started, use an area rug and pillows or a few chairs to set up a reading area where children can look at books after you have read them aloud. Display books so the children can see the covers. If there is no book-display stand, books can be placed standing up opened on a shelf or on a table. Some of the books displayed should reflect the current curriculum plan. The reading area usually works well in a corner, out of the traffic pattern, or otherwise protected from children's moving from area to area. It is considered a quiet area and thus should be away from the more active and noisy block areas and dramatic play areas. Remember to teach the children how to carefully handle books.

Remember that the reading area is a quiet area where children can get away from the stimulation of constant interaction with others. Therefore, it should be limited to only a few children at a time, or a child should be allowed to be alone there.

Selecting Appropriate Books

Review the following information about selecting books for preschoolers. Together, consider several books from the classroom library and evaluate the books using the following criteria. Ask the learner to use this information to evaluate up to 10 books from her classroom library, creating a separate evaluation sheet for each book. On the next visit, review these evaluation forms with her and offer additional suggestions.

Selecting Books for Preschoolers

Preschoolers are curious and eager to learn. Their world is full of new things to discover, including reading. With meaningful literacy experiences, young children will soon discover that letters make up words, the words make up sentences, and the sentences have meaning. Therefore, books can be very powerful to a preschooler. Literature builds upon the child's imagination, and the combination of illustrations, colors, and words on a page bring magic to the life of a preschooler.

Preschoolers enjoy books that bring humor to their everyday experiences and that teach them about the world they are anxious to discover. Talk about the author and illustrator of the book when you read to the children. Knowing that a book is the result of "real people" drawing pictures and writing words can serve as a wonderful motivation to learn to read, write, and appreciate the value of a picture. Talk about the objects in the book prior to reading it. Allow the children to share stories that relate to the story in the book.

When selecting books for preschoolers, look for books that:

- Include humor in reality.
- Introduce new words, but not so many that understanding is hindered.
- Include exaggeration.
- Explain the who's and why's.
- Build a connection between new and familiar facts.
- Prepare children for new experiences.
- Have colorful, bold, or realistic illustrations.
- Are stories that can come to life with puppets or other materials.
- Have good rhythm and repeated words.
- Are interactive, illustrate cause and effect, and pop up or have movement.
- Have predictable text for children to anticipate and join in the story.

Types of Books

Discuss the various types of books with the learner. Gather an assortment of books from the classroom library and ask her to group the books by the categories. Then help her to evaluate where there are gaps in types of books and make a plan to procure additional books to fill those needs.

- Counting, alphabet, and rhyming books, such as *One Fish, Two Fish, Red Fish, Blue Fish* by Dr. Seuss; *Chicka Chicka Boom Boom* by Bill Martin Jr.; and *Ashanti to Zula: African Traditions* by Margaret Musgrove
- Stories about children or animals, such as *A Chair for My Mother* by Vera B. Williams; *The Snowy Day* by Ezra Jack Keats; *Madeline* by Ludwig Bemelmans; *The Rainbow Fish* by Marcus Pfister; and *Owl Moon* by Jane Yolen
- Books that teach concepts, such as colors or shapes, such as *Mouse Paint* by Ellen Stoll Walsh; *Little Blue and Little Yellow* by Leo Lionni; and *The Village of Round and Square Houses* by Ann Grifalconi
- Predictable books, such as *The Napping House* by Audrey Wood and *Brown Bear, Brown Bear, What Do You See?* by Bill Martin Jr. and Eric Carle
- Folk tales and fables, such as *Why Mosquitoes Buzz in People's Ears: A West African Tale* by Verna Aardema; *Stone Soup* by Marcia Brown or by Heather Forest; and *The Bremen-Town Musicians* retold by Ilse Plume
- Biographies, such as *Me . . . Jane* by Patrick McDonnell and *Snowflake Bentley* by Jacqueline Briggs Martin
- Stories about everyday things, such as *Freight Train* by Donald Crews and the *I Spy* books by Jean Marzollo
- Stories about relationships and feelings, such as *Let's Be Enemies* by Janice May Udry; *Will I Have a Friend?* by Miriam Cohen; and *The Relatives Came* by Cynthia Rylant

Photo Documentation

Evaluate the reading center in the learner's classroom. Take a photo before, during, and after the technical assistance sessions. Ask the learner to use the photos to make a documentation chart. She can use the chart to involve the children in the changes being made for them.

Guidance in the Library Area

Supervising the Library Area

Model for the learner responsive interactions with children in the area. Pay careful attention to expanding children's concepts and skills and to enriching their language. After having her observe how you relate to the children, point out the reasons and rationale for your actions and your goals for the children.

What Do Children Need to Learn about the Library Area?

Brainstorm what children need to learn and do to use the library area appropriately. Help the learner develop a list of guidelines for children. For example, how many children can use the area at one time? Where do they put the books when they finish? How do they care for the books?

Increasing Literacy Opportunities

Ask the learner to make a list of all the ways literacy is incorporated into daily classroom activities. For example, reading books, dictating stories, using a weather chart, putting names on cubbies, labeling items in the classroom, and using music all have a literacy component. Work with the learner to identify places in the room or times in the day to add additional literacy opportunities.

Varying Stories

Ask the learner to brainstorm ways to use stories with children other than by reading books. For example, she might use a flannel board, tell or retell a story, or use puppets. Ask her to select one or two books, choose another way of presenting the story, and try it with the children.

Overcoming Barriers to an Effective Library Program

How to Obtain More Books

If the number of appropriate books is low and the budget is limited, help the learner find out how she can obtain more books. She might ask parents to donate books, she might find books at yard sales, or she might enroll in book clubs. Regular trips to the local library can also provide an endless supply of books. Ask her to contact the local library and inquire about what they do with books they are replacing. Libraries sometimes donate books that they are discarding or sell them inexpensively. In addition, she might want to establish a program for parents to donate a book when a child has a birthday or in recognition of holidays or special events. If so, help the learner make a list of books that she wants for the classroom library or provide a list of recommended books that she can give to the parents to select from, in order to get the books she needs and ensure they are appropriate.

Teacher-Made and Child-Made Books

Talk with the learner about making books for children and children making their own books. Show samples of some teacher-made and child-made books. Work with the learner to make a small book using construction paper, crayons, markers, white paper, and magazine or calendar pictures. Show her how to punch holes in the pages and bind the pages together with yarn. Point out that laminating these books will make them more durable. Have her make two or three of the books and share them with the children. Help her set up and conduct an activity for the children where they will make books together, and evaluate the activity afterward.

Here are some books that children might enjoy making:

- **Wordless Books:** The child draws pictures and then uses them to tell a story.
- **Dictated Stories:** The child draws a picture, and the teacher writes what the child says on the bottom of each page.
- **Zip Books:** The child selects pictures from a magazine or catalog, cuts them out, and inserts them in zip-closure bags. Pages are joined using a hole punch, hole re-enforcers, and notebook rings or yarn.

Holding a Book Drive

Book drives are an inexpensive way to build literacy resources. Advertise the book drive through fliers, the program's newsletter, or a local newspaper. Let the community know when and where they can donate new or gently used books. For maximum exposure, try to plan your book drive kickoff during a community or school fair or other celebration for maximum exposure. Let people know if they can drop off books year-round or only during the book-drive period. Be clear about the kinds of books and materials you need. You might even make up a wish list of the books you want.

Creating a Culture of Reading

Bulletin Board about Reading

Help the learner make a bulletin board or poster to let parents know about the importance of reading to their children. On the bulletin board, list about five reasons children benefit from being read to on a regular basis. The following are a few suggestions of what might be included in the bulletin board:

Read to Your Children Often

When you read books to your children, you are helping them:

- Increase their vocabularies
- Master the rhythm and patterns of language
- Recognize that the words in the book have meaning
- Understand the relationship of what is written to what is said
- Learn about the world around them
- Develop academic concepts such as math, science, social studies, and more
- Derive pleasure from reading

Reading Aloud Demonstration

Model reading a book to children while the learner observes. Following the observation, ask her to write down the answers to the following questions:

- How did the reader get the children's attention?
- Did the reader vary her vocal tone?
- How did the reader hold the book for children to see the pictures?
- Did the reader explain what words meant or help children understand words they likely would not otherwise understand?
- Did the reader involve the children in the story?
- How did the reader end the story?

Once she has answered all the questions, discuss the learner's answers as a way of helping her understand the skills required to read aloud effectively with children.

Reading Aloud

Ask the learner to select a book to read to children using the information on page 56. Review and discuss with the learner the following guidelines for reading aloud to children for tips on how to make the experience successful and pleasant for both the children and her. Observe her as she reads the book, and afterward answer the same questions from the preceding section that she answered when you read aloud to the children. Discuss your observations and offer suggestions for ongoing improvement.

Guidelines for Reading Aloud to Children

- Pick a comfortable place for reading. Cushions or pillows, good lighting, and a wide selection of appropriate books make the environment more appealing.
- Read to the smallest group possible. Small groups let more children become involved and encourage better conversations.
- Before reading the text, get to know the book with the children. Take time to look at the pictures together, discuss the objects in the book, and talk about the front and back of the book. Explain what authors and illustrators are.
- Allow children to talk about what they see in the book.
- When reading or telling a story, make it enjoyable by showing your enthusiasm. Change your voice for each character, ask good questions, and invite the children to predict what will happen next.

- Before you read the book, begin talking about it and invite other children to join the group. This way you don't lose the attention of the children sitting while waiting for others to come.
- Make predictions. Stop in the middle of the story and ask the children what they think will happen next or to make up their own ending.
- What do the children think? After reading a story to a small group or to an individual child, write the name of the book at the top of a piece of chart paper, and then ask the children to tell you about the story. Write each child's name and what each child says on the chart paper. Hang the paper on the wall in the reading center.
- Record favorite stories and place in the reading center for individual use later.
- Make it personal. Make up stories using the names of the children in the class. Have the children make up stories and tell them to you or each other.
- Act it out. Help the children make paper-bag costumes and act out a favorite story.
- Involve families. Have a special day for parents or grandparents to come read or conduct an activity with a class.

To Provide Rich Book Experiences:

- Teach children how to take care of the books.
- Put the book in the library area after you read it to the group. That way, children will then "read" it themselves.
- Don't spend too much time on each page. You want to hold their attention.
- Reading to children is a calming activity; it helps with transitions such as getting ready for lunch and rest time.
- Emphasize action words to keep children's attention.
- Give children many opportunities to predict what will happen next and to tell the story themselves.
- Recognize that there will be favorites that children will want to hear over and over.

Picture Books and Language Development: Keys to Success

- Helping children get to know the book before you read the text will help the children develop a love of books and learning.
- Allowing children to choose the books or the theme of the books will keep them interested and give the children more to discuss about the book or the topic.
- Asking open-ended questions encourages children to talk, predict, and experiment.
- Waiting patiently for children to answer questions will promote thinking skills.

When Children Have Developed a Love of Literature:

- They will return to the books that you have shared.
- They will look for books that are similar to their favorites.

- They will tell others about their favorites.
- They will act out, make up songs, or develop other activities that include their favorite stories and characters.
- They will freely choose to read or listen to stories.
- They will ask you to read more stories.

Equipping and Setting Up a Writing Center

Discuss the importance of a writing center and how it relates to the library area. Work with the learner to make a list of items that can go in the writing center:

- **Writing tools:** thick pencils, chalk and chalkboard, crayons, markers
- **Printing materials:** letter and design stencils, alphabet stamps, and ink pads
- **Paper of all types:** envelopes and stationery, index cards, unlined and lined paper, or tracing paper

Look at photos of writing centers or pictures of writing centers in catalogs. Help the learner to see how a writing center might be arranged and some items to include in it. Use the list below to guide the discussion:

- Display children's writing, including scribbles and lines!
- Provide sets of alphabet letters in wood, plastic, sandpaper, or magnetic materials.
- Include colored chalk and individual chalkboards.
- Provide a typewriter or computer keyboard or a clipboard, paper, and a pencil.
- Try a sand table or tray in the writing center.
- Feature book posters with labels in the center.
- Include an alphabet wall hanging, quilt, or rug.

Remember to set up a print-rich environment in other centers, with labels, signs, names, charts, sign-up sheets, bulletin boards, and other print materials.

Emergent Literacy and Environmental Print: Preschool Children and Writing

Children need to learn print awareness. They need to encounter print very early in life and have all kinds of interactive experiences with it. Discuss with the learner appropriate and inappropriate expectations of children's writing and the following emergent literacy experiences:

- Writing letters, words, or names of objects by scribbling on paper, sand tray, or in fingerpaint
- Printing the child's name or words with letters
- Writing letters, the child's name, or words on typewriter or computer
- Stamping letters to make the child's name or words
- Using playdough to form shapes, letters, words
- Playing with alphabet letters or blocks
- Using shaving cream to make scribbles, letters, and words
- Providing unlined paper, washable markers, pencils, crayons, and stencils for free writing

Learning to read and write emerges naturally in children given the proper conditions and encouragement. Just as children acquire language naturally and at their own pace, they can also acquire writing skills.

Putting It into Practice

What Is in the Library Area?

Using the new information and skills that are a result of the technical assistance, ask the learner to make a plan to add to her library area using the suggested supply list for a writing center on page 62. Help her make a plan to try something new.

Great Times for Reading

Ask the learner to identify some good times during the day for reading to children, and use the list that follows to help her to recognize additional times during the day when reading is appropriate. The times listed are good times both to read new books and to discuss books that have been read earlier.

At arrival time: Some children need a quiet transition time. It's a great time for parents to read to their child to help ease the transition from home to school.

During free time: Children love having a choice, and using books, puppets, and flannel board accessories is a wonderful activity for free time. Children can read to themselves, others, or stuffed animals.

During group time: A well-chosen story can be a wonderful addition to your circle time plans.

During bathroom waiting time or other transition time: While children are waiting for the restroom or other transitions, letting children look at or read books can help ease waiting time.

While you are preparing or cleaning up lunch: Children can read together or discuss books that have been read. You can add to the discussion as you work.

During and after meal times: Reading can occupy children who finish early and those who have difficulty waiting.

Before nap time: Reading a story can help the children relax and settle down for a good rest.

At the end of the day: What a great way to relax and prepare for the end of the day!

When older children want to read to younger children: Reading to others will help older children feel successful and will promote good reading habits. Older children love carefully selected chapter books. Read a chapter at a time and encourage comments and additions to the story.

Evaluation of Technical Assistance

Use the questions below as a worksheet or questionnaire to assess the learner's mastery of the technical assistance activities about reading centers:

1. What are reasons why a library area is an important part of a classroom?
2. What are guidelines for selecting books to use with young children?
3. How can you obtain an adequate amount of books if funds are limited?
4. How might children make their own books?
5. How can you include writing opportunities in a classroom?
6. What are some suggestions for reading aloud to young children?
7. What are additional times other than circle time for reading aloud?
8. How can you encourage families to read to their children?

Chapter 4 Technical Assistance:
The Music Area

The Value of Music

In most early childhood classrooms, the teachers and children sing a song or two at group or circle time. Many teachers use music to help children handle transitions. Families often sing lullabies and traditional rhymes to their young children, and at home and in the car, parents play recorded music they enjoy. Music certainly is present in the lives of many young children.

Yet, music may be underused in early childhood education, especially given the fact that the early years are prime times to capitalize on children's innate musical spontaneity, as well as to encourage their natural inclinations to sing, move, and play with sound.

Why Music May Not Get the Attention It Deserves

Ask the learner to think about the preceding paragraph and to suggest some reasons music might be underused in early childhood education. Use the following suggestions below as possibilities:

- Teachers may not recognize the value of music.
- Teachers may be intimidated because they feel they are not musically inclined.
- Teachers may not realize how music can enhance development and learning in other areas (language, math, reading, and so on).
- Teachers may think that music is only important for talented children.

Remembering Childhood

Ask the learner what she remembers about music from her own childhood. Ask her to share her feelings about her musical ability and how adults from her youth contributed to her current attitude toward music. Ask her to share some favorite songs from her childhood and to think about why they were her favorites. Help her determine the concepts or skills she may have learned from those favorite songs.

This chapter focuses on how to provide technical assistance that might help an adult learner understand the value of music for young children and to help the learner develop skills to incorporate more effective music activities into the daily routines. The activities in this chapter will help the learner:

- Select or find equipment to use for music experiences
- Evaluate the current use of music in her classroom and plan for improvement
- Support children's creativity in music and movement
- Recognize the importance of using music from other cultures
- Incorporate music even if she does not feel she is musically gifted

Why Include Music?

The Value of Music in the Classroom

A balanced, high-quality music program contributes to the objectives of helping children learn and develop socially, physically, mentally, emotionally, and spiritually. Discuss with the learner some of the ways she uses music in the classroom now. Ask her to think about why she uses music in those ways. Ask her to describe some of the benefits to children of using music in the classroom. Use the following information to lead the discussion.

Music Helps Children:

- Develop a sense of rhythm.
- Improve physical coordination.
- Learn and improve social skills.
- Extend their attention spans.
- Expand their vocabulary.
- Enlarge their capacity for pure enjoyment.

More Reasons for Music

- Music is a universal language.
- Music encourages laughter, creativity, freedom, and movement.
- Music can teach concepts such as colors or numbers.
- Music experiences are tied to the understanding of math.
- Music can increase physical activity.
- Music can relieve tension, lift the spirits, and soothe.
- Most important: It's fun!

Emphasize how music can be used at any time during the day, not just at group time or music time or in the music areas. Look for songs that can be used during morning greeting, group time, center time, rest time, and departure. Also discuss how transitions are important times of the day and are often challenging and must be planned for. Point out how music can be used throughout the day to help smooth transitions. Talk about examples of songs that are good for transitions.

Show the learner examples of props and the songs they go with and some samples of homemade musical instruments. Ask her to select three or four of the ideas to use. The next time you meet with the learner, talk about her experience with using songs, instruments, and props.

Brainstorm other possibilities for the music program with the learner. For example, she might ask a member of a symphony orchestra, a local band member, or any musician to visit the classroom. However, make sure to emphasize that all guests should know what to expect from the class (for example, how long the children can sit still to listen). Preparing the guests and the children ensures the best possible outcome.

Why Music Now?

Point out to the learner that music is especially important in the early years and why creating a culture of including music is important. Use the list below to guide the discussion:

Importance of Music in the Early Childhood Classroom

- Music stimulates the brains of young children.
- By including a variety of music types and musical instruments in the environment, you can expand the experiences of young children.
- Music exposes children to pitch, rhythm, and pattern, encouraging children to discriminate sounds and identify familiar patterns.
- Singing or playing in a group builds a sense of teamwork.
- Movement with music can enhance physical development of large and small motor skills through singing.

A Universal Language

Ask the learner to discuss why music is considered to be a universal language. Discuss how the rhythm and beat of music speak to all people—young and old alike, people from all countries and cultures. Point out how everyone responds to the beat and rhythm of music, and most cultures enjoy dancing and singing. Thus, we can enjoy music even if we do not understand the words.

Explain the importance of including music from the cultures of the families in the learner's class or program as well as other cultures. Listening to songs in other languages exposes children to the concepts of differences in languages. Discuss with the learner examples of how to include music activities from the children's cultures or other cultures relevant to the program's themes and units.

Also discuss songs in other languages that the learner might know. Two common examples are "Frère Jacques," and "De Colores." Ask the learner to share any songs from other cultures that she knows.

Play several different types of music (fast, slow, classical, patriotic, music from another culture, and so on) and ask the learner how she responds to the music. Ask questions such as the following:

- How did you feel during the fast music?
- Did you want to clap your hands, play an instrument, or stomp your feet?

- How did you feel during the slow music? Was it soothing and relaxing?
- Did the classical music bring images to mind? What did you think about during the classical music?

What Music Teaches

Look through the supply of music in the classroom. Ask the learner to identify songs or music that can teach children about the following:

- Following directions
- Patterns and listening skills
- Language skills
- Cultures
- Cognitive skills, such as counting, rhyming words, and color recognition

Music Teaches Listening

Offer some musical instruments to the learner. Keep a pair of rhythm sticks for yourself. Pick a beat and tap it out with the rhythm sticks. Let the learner copy your beat with the other instruments. Then ask her to tap a beat and you can clap, snap fingers, make up words, or move to the beat. Point out that echoing a pattern is an important listening skill.

Providing Music Experiences for Children

Review of How Music Can Be Used in the Preschool Classroom

Review with the learner how to use music in the preschool classroom and the benefits for children. Discuss the value of music: how it can be used as a transition, as a way to provide an active break, and as a way to develop children's small motor coordination and listening skills.

What Do Children Need to Learn about Using the Music Area?

Brainstorm with the learner what children need to learn and do in order to use the music area appropriately. Help the learner develop a list of guidelines for children in the area. For example, guidelines might include how many children can use the area at one time, where they use the music instruments, and where they put the items when they finish.

Setting Up a Music Area

What Do I Need for a Music Area?

Using the information in the following Essentials for a Music Area list, help the learner evaluate what she already has that can help improve her existing music area, or if she does not already have one, help her establish a music area. Also, offer suggestions of inexpensive items that she can get or make quickly. Show her examples of rhythm instruments both purchased and teacher-made, and provide time for the learner to explore the musical instruments. Discuss the concepts that the instruments will help the children discover and how children can use accessories like scarves to make the music more fun.

Essentials for a Music Area

- Music to listen to on an electronic player or computer
- Recorders for individual songs or creations
- Musical instruments such as bells, triangles, rhythm sticks, wood blocks, tambourines, maracas, guitar or stringed instrument, piano or autoharp
- Props for movement such as scarves, flowing cloths, long skirts (not long enough to trip on)
- Space that allows for movement
- A wide variety of music, such as children's songs, classical music, jazz, rock-and-roll that is appropriate for young children, reggae, rhythm and blues, music characteristic of many cultures, songs in many languages, lullabies, rap that is appropriate for young children, folk songs, and country and western

Photo Evaluation

Show the learner photos of music areas and discuss the pros and cons of each. Review the handout, **The Music Center** on page 146 with the learner, and brainstorm items that she might purchase or move from another area to improve on or establish a music area. Also, review a school supply catalog together and consider several items from the catalog that might enrich the music program and area. Ask her to think of activities that she could plan for each item and how she might use the items that she chooses.

Assessing a Music Program

Use the following information to assess the learner's music area and music activities and to plan for improvement.

Assessing Your Music Program

- Is there a variety of musical experiences and activities available?
- Is music an integrated part of the program, using recordings, individual and group singing, instruments, creative movements, and dancing?
- Does the supply of music include a variety for quiet listening and rhythmic activity, as well as songs to sing?
- Is there open space for children to move about freely for creative movement?
- Are there props, such as scarves or streamers, to dance with?
- Are there musical instruments available for experimentation with sound and creation with music?

- Are different types of music used, such as music from many cultures?
- Is the emphasis on enjoyment rather than on performance?
- Is music used as a motivator for other tasks, such as cleanup, and during transitional time?
- Is music used throughout the day, especially at beginnings and endings, transitions, for calming down, or an opportunity to get up and move?
- Is music expanded into general play?
- Are music experiences broadened to outdoors?
- Is there a wide a variety of musical experiences and activities, such as the following:
  - Singing songs with children while they transition from group time to snack
  - Playing soft music at nap time
  - Singing a good morning song
  - Singing a cleanup song
  - Having children play rhythm instruments to different kinds of music during circle time
  - Bringing musical instruments outside
  - Allowing children to freely access the music center
- Are there sufficient musical instruments available for at least half of the children in the class to play at once?

Types of Music and Musical Instruments

Discuss with the learner the various types of music that can be used with young children. Gather an assortment of music from the classroom, and have her select the ones she has used successfully. Then help her to evaluate where there are gaps in the types of music that are available and make a plan to procure additional music to fill those needs.

Guiding and Enriching the Music Area

Supervising the Music Area

Model for the learner responsible interactions with children in the music area. Pay careful attention to expanding children's concepts and skills as they use the materials. After she observes how you relate to the children, discuss your reasons and goals.

Music and Creative Movement

Discuss with the learner the importance of creative movement with young children, and work with her to make a list of reasons for including movement activities. Play lively music and let her enjoy moving to the beat. Demonstrate the use of some items to be used in creative movement activities, such as scarves, streamers, or ribbons. Ask the learner to make a list of other items children can use while they dance and move creatively. If no props are available, help her write a note requesting some from parents or make a plan to purchase some. Use the following information as the basis for the discussion.

How Adults Can Support Children's Creativity in Music and Movement

1. Respect creative play.
2. Provide a wide variety of activities and materials to expand children's imaginations.
3. Provide space and time.
4. Provide problem-solving opportunities.
5. Respect the process as much, if not more than, the product.

Remember: Children are natural musicians. When they hear music, they move to it! Play lively music and let the learner enjoy moving to the beat. Point out how important movement is and how children can enjoy creative movement in many ways, such as singing, dancing, or moving to music.

To demonstrate how easy it is to combine music and movement, ask the learner to take a song or chant that does not typically include movements and make up movement and actions for the song or chant. Suggest a song if she cannot come up with one. Sing or play "The Erie Canal," "You Are My Sunshine," "It's Not Easy Being Green," "Lazy Mary," or "This Old Man" and do the actions with the learner.

Another way to add creativity is to ask her to make up some new movements for songs that already have common motions associated with them, such as "The Itsy Bitsy Spider," "I'm a Little Teapot," "Five Little Speckled Frogs," or "The Wheels on the Bus."

Review the music recordings that are available in the learner's classroom. Select some that will be good to use for movement. Ask the learner to evaluate why these will be good as movement activities. Ask her to try some and give feedback.

Music from Many Cultures

Review the music in the learner's classroom to look for music from other cultures and in other languages. If none are available, provide some suggestions for purchases, or borrow some from a library. Discuss the value of using music from cultures around the world.

Point out how children can be helped to see that although the words might be different in another language, the tune may be familiar. If possible, find two versions of a familiar song, each in a different language. Two possibilities to demonstrate are "The Hokey Pokey" and "Frère Jacques."

Overcoming Barriers to Including Music

Making Musical Instruments

Use the handout **Making Musical Instruments** on page 147, and select one or more of the items to help the learner make. Help her select several more to make before you visit again. On the next visit, discuss her progress and additional items to make.

So You Can't Sing and Don't Play an Instrument

While children may all be natural musicians, not all adults may be. However, even if the learner doesn't consider herself to be particularly musically inclined, this does not mean she is not capable of providing meaningful, fun, and effective music experiences. Share the following information with the learner, and answer any questions she has. Use the information as a way to discuss how to incorporate music into the curriculum if a person feels that she is not a good singer. Point out that music should be used for the expression and joy it brings rather than perfection of performance.

Easy Ways to Bring Music into the Classroom

- Even if you can't sing, sing anyway. The children do not care, and they will have fun regardless.
- Purchase or make simple rhythm instruments, such as drums, rhythm sticks, bells, and wood blocks. You can also make instruments out of objects around the classroom or from home, such as shakers, tambourines, kazoos, sandpaper, coffee-can drums, and shoebox guitars.
- Record or purchase different types of music (classical, jazz, pop, new age, zydeco, and so on) and play them for the children.
- Have children draw what they think is happening in the music or move however the music makes them feel.
- Have children make up a story about what they imagine is happening when they listen to instrumental music.
- Dance to different types of music (fast and active, slow and relaxing) using scarves or streamers.
- Explore the world of sound by recording familiar, everyday sounds such as a telephone ringing, a door closing, a vacuum cleaning, and water running. Listen to these sounds, and have the children guess what the sounds are. You can also cut out pictures of the objects that make each sound and have the children match the objects to the sound. For even more fun, have them "act out" the sound—even play a game where children make up an action and the others have to guess what the sound is.
- Encourage the children to explore their own "instrument" they carry with them every day: themselves! Have them experiment with different sounds their bodies can make (click, snap, clap, stomp, swish, and so on).

> ### A Cautionary Note
>
> Music should not be played in the background all day long. When music is always playing in the background, it adds to the noise pollution in the classroom, and children tune it out or they are forced to talk louder. Point out to the learner that music should be featured at various times, such as a march tune to go outdoors, a quiet song at rest time, and a happy, lively song to go along with movement.

Creating a Culture of Music

Parent Letter about Music: Help the learner write a letter to let parents know about the importance of music for young children. In the letter, encourage families to sing and dance with their children. Point out how music can develop listening skills, recognition of rhyming words, rhythm, and pure enjoyment.

Music Poster: Help the learner make a poster listing the value of music to help parents understand why the learner incorporates music into her curriculum plans.

Rhythm Instruments: Observe the learner using rhythm instruments if she has them in her classroom. If not, demonstrate and assist her in making some. Model using the instruments with a small group of children. After she observes how you use the instruments with the children, point out your reasons and goals.

Putting It into Practice

Adding Music to Daily Plans

Ask the learner why and when she currently uses music in her program, and encourage her to think about other times she could use music. Ask her to write the ideas on an index card. Discuss how the learner can plan for music experiences throughout the day. Show the learner examples of daily plans so she can see how music can be used at various times during the day:

- Choose a song or group of related songs appropriate to the ages of the children;
- Prepare discussion topics and questions to ask;
- Collect books related to the song;
- Prepare activities related to topic of the song.

Discuss how to use excellent music in many styles. Play several types of music and discuss how they might be used—for example, playing soft music at nap time.

Discuss with the learner the following questions: What musical experiences does a young child want and need? What do the children in your program enjoy? Point out that she should not expect all children to respond to music in the same way. Give some examples of child responses, such as clapping to a song, singing to a song, and even dancing to a song. It is important to allow children to respond individually according to their feelings, not necessarily in a uniform manner.

I Write the Songs: Point out to the learner that she and the children can sing a familiar tune but make up new words. Give the learner an example of a made-up song to use for transition time by using a familiar tune with new words; discuss what time of day this song might be used.

Then make up motions for the song and tell what the song is teaching or demonstrating.

Creative Movement

Ask the learner to describe some of the ways she uses music in creative movement. Present some or all of the ideas in the list below. Discuss how she might incorporate these activities into her program. Point out that creative movement is a good way to give children a chance to move around during the day between quieter activities. This movement can be a break at group time or an alternative for when they are unable to go outdoors. Ask the learner to try some of the following ideas. The next time you meet with her, discuss what happened when she tried the idea or ideas she selected.

Bedtime and Awake Time: Shake a shaker gently and sing or chant: "Go to sleep. Put on your pajamas. Get under the covers. Goodnight." Then tap a lively beat on two rhythm sticks and chant: "I'm gonna jump with my toes, jump with my feet, jump with my nose, jump with my knees, jump with my bones, jump with my feet, jump with my heart, beat, beat, beat!" Then switch to the shaker and start again. The children fake sleep and then jump up and down to the beat.

Paper Plate Skate: Give each child two paper plates, one for each foot. Turn on some classical music (music from *The Nutcracker* works great), and have the children skate around the room to the music. Preschoolers love this activity.

Rain, Rain, Time to Play: Stand in the middle of the room with a large closed umbrella. The children march, hop, skip, or move any other way around the room. When you open up the umbrella, that is the signal that the rain has started and the children have to run to a spot under the umbrella to keep dry until the sun comes out again and they can play.

Music Art: Cover a table with a large piece of newsprint. Play music. Have the children walk around the table with marker or crayon in hand, making movements on the paper to the beat of the music. Vary the types of music played, or play a stop-and-go "freeze" game. This idea combines art, music, and movement together. Ask children to draw what the music sounds like.

Feather Dance: Take a bag of colored craft feathers to a large, open area. Give each child one to "feather dance" with. While the music is playing, tell the children that they are to keep the feather in the air by blowing it. After awhile, throw the whole bag of feathers in the air and have the children run around gathering up their own little bunches. For cleanup, give each child a color of feather to pick up.

Evaluation of Technical Assistance

Use the questions below as a worksheet or questionnaire to assess the learner's mastery of the technical assistance activities about the music area:

1. What are reasons why music is an important part of a curriculum for young children?
2. What are some guidelines for equipping and setting up a music area?
3. How can you support creativity in music and movement?
4. How can children make and use their own musical instruments?
5. How can a teacher who feels she cannot sing provide quality music experiences?
6. What are some suggestions of how to include music in daily routines?

Chapter 5 Technical Assistance:
Outdoor Play

Why Outdoor Play?

The value and importance of outdoor play is a growing focus in early childhood education. This chapter contains technical activities to help an adult learner understand the value of outdoor play and to support learning in all domains during regular outdoor time.

The activities in this chapter will provide opportunities for the learner to:

- Recognize the vital role that outdoor playtime holds in young children's development;
- Identify the ways that outdoor time contributes to various skills and competencies;
- Examine ways to provide appropriate guidance to support safety, reduce conflicts, and encourage cooperation;
- Support children's creativity in the outdoors; and
- Locate free or inexpensive ways to provide variety in outdoor play.

Remembering Childhood

Begin by making two lists—one by you and one by the learner—of outdoor games that you played as a child. Evaluate why the games were popular then and, perhaps, for other generations. Discuss which of the games children might enjoy today.

Discuss how the learner feels about the outdoors by asking her the following questions:

- What do you remember enjoying most about playing outdoors when you were a child? What did you enjoy least?
- How much time did you spend outside?
- What are your favorite memories of play, and where did they take place?
- What sights, sounds, textures, and tastes do you remember?
- As an adult, what do you enjoy most about being outdoors? What do you enjoy least?
- Is there is a difference in how you felt as a child and how you feel as an adult? What is the difference?

- If you don't enjoy the outdoors now as much as you did as a child, is there something that could make you like the outdoors more?
- Why do you think children do not spend as much time outdoors today as children did at other times?

Discuss with the learner the reasons why children spend less time outdoors today. Some ideas include the following:

- Lack of time and space;
- Real or perceived dangers;
- Competition from television and electronic entertainment;
- Additional schoolwork or travel time to and from school; and
- Lack of neighborhood children to play with.

How Does Outdoor Play Contribute to Children's Development?

To assess the learner's knowledge of the benefits of outdoor play, ask her open-ended questions about why it is desirable for children to go outdoors regularly. Use the following information about how outdoor play contributes to children's development as a guide for discussion if the learner has difficulty making suggestions.

How Outdoor Play Contributes to Children's Development

Physical Development

- Develops and refines large- and small-muscle skills
- Develops eye-hand coordination
- Improves balance and increasing spatial awareness
- Allows for exploration and discovery of what their bodies can do
- Improves health through exercise and being in the fresh air
- Increases stamina and physical endurance through activities such as climbing, running, jumping

Cognitive Development

- Develops language and communication skills—increases vocabulary as they participate in games and invent, modify, and enforce rules of games
- Enables decision making, planning and carrying though ideas, and solving problems
- Encourages identification and observation of many cause-and-effect relationships in nature
- Allows for the experience of seeing changes in the weather and seasons
- Develops an understanding of math concepts through classification, measuring, or counting as children keep score and count in games they play

Social and Emotional Development

- Builds cooperation in group games and activities
- Allows for sharing and taking turns on equipment, and negotiating compromises

- Encourages expressions of creativity
- Develops a sense of pride in their accomplishments
- Develops independence and self-esteem as they learn to use equipment and gain confidence in their physical abilities
- Most important: It's fun!

Use the information in the preceding section as a guide to coach the learner on recognizing the value of outdoor play in children's development, and ask her to use this information to begin compiling an ongoing list of additional ways she observes that outdoor play contributes to children's development.

Observation Exercise

Ask the learner to observe a group of children playing outdoors for at least 15 minutes, and note the ways in which the children's play contributes to their development, such as coordination, or to their understanding of concepts like *up* and *down*. Ask her to complete the **Outdoor Observation Form** on page 149 and to offer specific examples when documenting her observations.

Take a Walk Outdoors

Take a walk outdoors with the learner and help her to observe and identify the opportunities children have to experience nature. Ask her to consider what additional opportunities the setting could provide if some changes were made. Summarize the exercise by making the following points:

- Outdoors, children have unique opportunities to observe nature firsthand, to explore, and to enjoy the freedom of space and movement.
- The outdoors is an evolving learning environment containing many raw materials, such as grass, dirt, and water, which are naturally appealing to children.
- The early childhood field is recognizing the many benefits derived from exposure to nature and the disadvantages that result from children not having such opportunities.
- Nature can be soothing, calming, and relaxing.

Paying Attention to Nature

Ask the learner to select one of the following topics or a similar topic, introduce it to the children, and then observe the children's interest in it. Below are some possibilities to observe and explore:

Science Opportunities

- Rainwater evaporating
- Clouds moving in the sky
- Leaves blowing
- Tree limbs bending

Classification Skills

- Finding likenesses in plants
- Rock or seed collections to sort
- Leaves to press in books

Aesthetic Appreciation

- The colors of the flowers, trees, and plants
- The many textures
- How the seasons and weather change

Help the learner discover and identify other ways to help children pay attention to and value nature.

Evaluating the Playground

Using the **Outdoor Safety Checklist** on page 150 or a checklist based on your state regulations, help the learner assess her program's playground for safety in layout, equipment, and supervision. If any hazards are identified, help the learner create a plan to eliminate the hazards. If no hazards are present, look for problems in traffic flow, a need for better equipment, or more variety in the types of equipment.

Mapping the Playground

Work with the learner to draw a map of the outdoor play area if she wishes to relocate equipment to improve the layout; help her plan a layout that will improve any of the problems. Because moving large, permanently installed equipment can be expensive, focus on making a long-range plan and on the items that the learner can control.

Reviewing Licensing and Quality Standards

Working with the learner, use your state licensing standards section for playgrounds, Early Childhood Environment Rating Scale, or the National Association for the Education of Young Children (NAEYC) guidelines to compare your state's minimum standards with those that define quality. Help the learner complete an action plan using the handout on page 126 to move from minimum standards to a higher level of quality.

What Do I Need Outdoors?

Review what outdoor equipment is currently available and help the learner make a list of items that could improve the opportunities for children with a goal of including equipment for all developmental domains and needs. Use the following information as a starting point to suggest additional equipment.

Suggested Play Areas Outdoors

Playground Equipment Areas

- Climbing structures, balance beams, platforms, ramps, and other stationary active-play equipment
- Conventional swings and/or tire swings
- Slides

Riding Area

- Tricycles, wagons, and other riding toys
- Signs, directional arrows, orange cones
- Prop boxes to stimulate creative play with the riding toys, such as fire station, mail delivery, police station

Quiet Play Area

- Crayons, paper, sidewalk chalk
- Books, music players, and rhythm instruments
- Paints and easels
- Quiet board games
- Tarpaulin, blanket, or sheet to make shade or a playhouse

Sand and Water Area

- Plastic buckets, bowls, and pails with handles
- Shovels and scoops of all sizes
- Funnels and sifters
- Plastic pitchers and jugs
- Sand or water pumps and wheels
- Plastic trucks, cars, fire engines, trains, and boats
- Plastic people and animals

Establishing Interest Centers Outside

Expanding Children's Outside Play

Discuss with the learner how many indoor activities, such as those for dramatic play, art, or music, can also be set up outdoors. Work with her to determine which activities will work well outdoors in her program. Some activities that stimulate active play, such as dramatic play, work better outdoors, where children have more room and more freedom to be louder than is desirable indoors. Help the learner to see the value of adding some of the following interest areas to the outdoors. Help her plan what she needs and how she can set up and supervise the areas. Also brainstorm guidelines and how to introduce the outdoor area.

Dramatic Play: Ask the learner to think about what she might do to provide dramatic play opportunities for children when they are outdoors. For example, old appliance boxes can be decorated by the children and transformed into boats, planes, automobiles, castles, or forts. In addition to dress-up clothes, blankets, sheets, and other realistic props can enhance the play environment. Dramatic play outdoors can make use of tricycles and wagons as cars, trucks, and other vehicles that are part of the children's play themes.

Music and Movement: Encourage the learner to incorporate music into outdoor activities with the children; an indoor environment with its space and noise limitations sometimes constrains these activities. Ask her to brainstorm how she might include music in her outdoor time. For example, she might let children dance and move to music with scarves. Children can make music using outdoor materials; sticks on metal or wooden playground equipment make very interesting sounds.

Art: Ask the learner to consider some art activities that will work well outdoors. When you conduct art activities outside, spills and messes are less of a concern; discuss some of the following examples of messy art activities that might be better outdoors.

- Easel painting can be done outdoors where spills are not a concern
- Fingerpainting, which can be done on a table to make it easy to clean up
- Taping paper on a storage building or using clothespins to attach cardboard to a fence and letting the children paint
- Using a variety of types and sizes of brushes and papers
- Letting the children take off their shoes and walk in paint, then onto paper to make interesting designs
- Filling a squirt bottle with thin liquid tempera paint and letting the children spray it onto paper
- Decorating the sidewalks or other concrete surfaces with colored chalk
- "Fence weaving" scraps of ribbon, yarn, streamers, or fabric through the fence openings

Library: Explain that outdoor time can offer a balance of active and quiet activities. Point out that nature's soft sounds can be soothing and conducive to reading, and ask the learner to identify a place on the playground where a book area might be set up. Suggest that she find a shady area if possible. Ask her what she could take outdoors to create a reading area—one possibility is a beach towel. For outdoor reading, books selected might relate to outside experiences.

Science and Math: Brainstorm with the learner some ideas about science and math experiences outdoors. Point out that outdoor time is a great time to go on a nature walk. The following are a few suggestions about science and math activities outdoors to help the learner get started:

- Leading a scavenger hunt and having the children look for particular objects
- Sorting, classifying, and counting out sets of rocks or acorns
- Counting in jumping rhymes
- Looking at flowers and counting the petals and leaves
- Using a magnifying glass to look closely at the ground

Sand and Water Play: Have the learner make a plan to establish or improve a water-play area. Ask her to design at least two water-play experiences that could take place outdoors. What items will she need? Where will she set it up? What guidance will be needed? If she needs some ideas to get started, use the following suggestions:

- Hoses and sprinklers can be used during warm weather. Provide cups, buckets, and other plastic containers for water play. Set up a "car wash" and let the children wash the riding equipment!
- Instead of filling the water table with the hose, let the children fill it with little jars and buckets from the faucet. This extends the filling and pouring activity and helps children work together on a common task.
- Set up a small wading pool full of water on warm days. Add assorted items for filling and pouring.
- Let the children use water and paintbrushes or rollers to "paint" on buildings or fences.
- Put two dishpans side by side. Fill one with water, adding food coloring to make it more visible. Challenge the child to transfer the water from one tub to the other using a meat baster.

- Fill plastic containers, such as margarine tubs, with water and a little food coloring and freeze. Unmold in the water table outside and place in a sunny spot.
- Provide a dishpan filled with water, bars of soap, washcloths, towels, and dolls for bath-time fun.
- Wash doll clothes in dishpans full of water and mild detergent. Hang on a clothesline to dry.
- Let children use sponges and scrub brushes to wash classroom chairs.

Guidance for Outdoor Play

If discipline is an issue outdoors, ask the learner to consider using the following strategies to remove environmental contributions to discipline matters and to improve overall guidance.

Traffic Patterns: Ask the learner to observe and track the traffic patterns the children use on the playground. Identify where children disturb other children's activities or where their movement creates hazards, such as walking near swings. Using the information gathered, make a plan to relocate some items or provide barriers to create better traffic flow. Use graph paper to plan the layout of the playground to scale.

Review Outdoor Policies, Practices, and Schedules: Ask the learner to discuss with the director the program's outdoor policies or practices. If none exist, or if they have not been revised in some time, ask the learner to help the director begin developing or revising the policies. For example, practices should include a regular time for each classroom to use the playground, guidelines for supervision and ratios, how the equipment is used, what to do about inclement weather, and responsibilities about removing or reporting hazards or problems. The next time you meet with the learner, review the results of these meetings.

Sensory Play: Sensory activities, which are relaxing for children, can sometimes reduce discipline problems. If sensory play is lacking, discuss with her the value of sensory play, such as sand and water play, and help her develop a plan for adding these types of sensory activities.

Overcoming Barriers to Outdoor Play
Solutions to Problems with Using the Outdoor Environment

Review state or quality standards and the requirements for outdoor play. With the learner, brainstorm all the problems or barriers that get in the way of making the outdoors a safe, rich, and fun environment for learning. Ask her to identify and propose solutions to the problems. The following are examples of some possible problems and solutions:

- **Too cold on many days:** Wear appropriate clothing; keep active outdoors; provide extra jackets for children and adults.
- **Too hot on many days:** Look for ways to provide shade and a lot of water activities.

- **Not enough time:** Schedule outdoor time as part of the daily routine. Consider the value of the learning opportunities outdoors.
- **Not enough teachers to supervise:** Recognize that teachers need a break, but not during outdoor time. Coordinate outdoor schedules with other classes to maximize supervision.
- **Not enough to do outdoors:** Bring some indoor activities outside. Teach the children group games, provide inexpensive items such as balls, and set up an obstacle course using recycled and donated items.
- **Parents do not want children to get dirty:** Make sure upon enrollment that parents know about the policies related to dress: that the children will be going outdoors regularly and that the children need to bring in extra clothing during cold or wet weather.

Emphasize the importance of planning outdoor play—it helps to overcome barriers, proving to the learner that the outdoors is as valuable a learning environment as the indoors.

Ask the learner about what to do when the weather is too bad to go outdoors. Help her select or develop some gross motor activities that can be done indoors. The children do not get the exercise they need if the caregiver sets up a video for them to watch, or if the caregiver plans quiet activities that do not promote gross motor development.

Teaching Children to Use Equipment Safely

Model interactions for the learner on how to assist children in using equipment safely. For example, explain to children why they should not go down a slide headfirst, why they should not

walk too close to swings, why they should hold on tightly when climbing, and so on. Discuss your interactions with the learner.

Evaluating Equipment Needs

Evaluate the playground relative to the number of play spaces. Make a plan for adding more if needed. Using a list of popular outdoor equipment or a catalog of playground equipment, along with lists the learner creates, help her determine which items are needed to enrich the playground. Help her select what she needs, and prepare a "wish list" of items she would like when funds are available.

Creative—and Inexpensive—Ideas for Playground Materials and Activities

If you and the learner have determined that the outdoor area lacks materials or equipment, use the following information to help the learner implement meaningful outdoor activities that use only inexpensive or free equipment.

- Make an obstacle course using rope, chalk, blocks, tires, sawhorses, boxes, hoops, or boards.
- Provide paper and crayons for children to make rubbings from brick, asphalt, fence, and other textures.
- Provide large boxes for forts or houses.
- Use a sheet or blanket for parachute play. The children hold onto the edges to lift it and hold it up for other children to run inside and out. Try moving to music during the activity.
- Use rope to tie a tarpaulin, blanket, or sheet to a fence or structure and make a tent.
- Ask the children to close their eyes and talk about what they hear or feel.
- Balance on a piece of wood, blocks, or a line drawn with chalk.
- Toss beanbags filled loosely (for easy gripping) into boxes and baskets.
- Make pinwheels and scarves for streaming on windy days.
- Make foam blocks cut from large foam mattress pieces for the children to use for building.
- Bury some small items—such as plastic dinosaurs, seashells, or pinecones—in a sand table or large dishpan filled with sand or another sensory material before the children go out to play. Let the children discover the items on their own. Provide small plastic cups for their treasures.
- Set up bubble-blowing with large coat-hanger hoops to make large bubbles. Make cube-shaped bubble wands by threading pipe cleaners through straws and connect to make a cube with a handle. Additional bubble-makers include berry baskets, spoons with holes in them, funnels, plastic straws, pipe cleaners formed into hoops, plastic rings, new flyswatters, and plastic clothes hangers. Let children use their imaginations.
- Tie items—such as chimes and pie tins—to trees to make interesting sounds in the wind.
- Place rubber floor mats, woven floor mats, throw rugs, soft blankets, vinyl, or other items with interesting textures on the ground to sit on.
- Use a box decorated like a gas pump, play money or pretend credit cards, and riding toys to make gas stations.
- Set up a small tent or make one from a sheet for pretend camping. Offer play cooking utensils and dishes, pillows for sleeping bags, and let children find sticks for a pretend campfire.
- Turn music on and have the children ride around the tricycle path. When you turn the music off, they must stop. Start the music for them to ride again.
- Suggest that children design a tricycle obstacle course or decorate tricycles and have a parade.
- Paint small stones gold and have a treasure hunt. When the children are not around, bury the stones in the sand and let the children search for buried treasure.

- Let children make a target on a paper plate and attach it to a tree. Children can then use plastic squirt bottles filled with water to try to hit the target.
- On a warm day, let children wear swimsuits and paint their bodies with washable tempera paints. Provide an unbreakable mirror so they can check their progress. They can rinse off with a hose when finished.
- Use clothespins to attach paper to a fence and let children paint outdoors. For variety, paint with spray bottles filled with water and food coloring.
- Let children collect nature objects, such as leaves, sand, and pine needles, to glue on cardboard in an arrangement as an individual or cooperative group project.
- Plant a garden.
- Have children practice rolling a ball into a box at the bottom of the slide.
- Ask the children to see how many different things they can do with hoops or balls.

Putting It into Practice

Books to Support Outdoor Play: Look through the classroom books for stories that generate ideas for outdoor play. Discuss with the learner how reading these books to the children prior to outdoor time with the necessary materials available can generate new outdoor activities or a renewed interest in playground time. For example, reading books about seasons, gardens, trees, outdoor work, or children using their imaginations in the outdoors can stimulate activities. The following are just a few suggestions:

- *All the World* by Liz Garton Scanlon
- *A Box Can Be Many Things* by Dana Meachen Rau
- *The Gardener* by Sarah Stewart
- *Red Sings from Treetops: A Year in Colors* by Joyce Sidman
- *Tip Tip Dig Dig* by Emma Garcia
- *This Is the Tree: A Story of the Baobab* by Miriam Moss

Recording Progress: Work with the learner to make a scrapbook using photos of various playground activities with captions explaining why the activity is important. Have her share the scrapbook with both the children and the parents.

Using the Outdoors Creatively: Ask the learner to think about creating a dramatic play theme outdoors. What materials should be provided? How would she get children involved? What type of guidance should be provided?

Use the following questions to help her think of other possibilities:

- What can you bring outside to create an interesting environment if you have little equipment?
- What are some free or inexpensive items that you might add to your playground?
- What types of music activities might you do outdoors?
- What items can you use to create an obstacle course?

Stress that an important part of the teacher's role outdoors is to help children use the environment in creative and imaginative ways. Emphasize the following points:

- The teacher helps create the outdoor environment by providing props for children's play.
- Any outdoor space that is available can be used creatively when you plan for the environment.
- The outdoor environment naturally changes throughout the year, providing many opportunities to create an exciting learning environment.

Resources on Outdoor Play: Work with the learner to conduct an Internet search on preschool outdoor play and find at least one of the following:

- More books related to outdoor play for children
- Other reasons, beyond what is found in these assignments, why outdoor play is essential to children
- Other outdoor activities that she considers to be of value to the children in her class
- Information about the benefits and importance of children and nature

Explain how to evaluate a website to make sure it is likely to have accurate information. Ask her to create a document that describes the information that she found and includes a citation of the website where she found the information.

Evaluation of Technical Assistance

Use the questions below as a worksheet or questionnaire to assess the learner's mastery of the technical assistance activities for outdoor play:

1. What are some ways outdoor play contributes to children's development in each domain?
2. What are some barriers to good outdoor environments?
3. What are some tips for assuring children's safety outdoors?
4. How can you support creativity in the outdoors?
5. What are typical indoor activities that can also take place outdoors?
6. What are suggestions of free or inexpensive items that can be used outdoors?
7. What are some objections to outdoor time, and how might you address those objections?

Chapter 6 Technical Assistance:
The Science Area

Why Science for Young Children?

When asked about science activities, many early childhood educators express concern that they are not doing enough. Many fail to recognize the science experiences or opportunities that arise throughout the day. This chapter is designed to help adult learners recognize the science already occurring in their classrooms and the many other opportunities for providing science on a regular basis. This chapter will provide experiences for the adult learner to:

- Build an understanding of what science is and what it is not;
- Identify activities that are appropriate for preschool children;
- Learn to support children's inquisitiveness and desire to understand aspects of science;
- Identify materials to use in the science area and provide guidance about how to make the materials easily accessible to the children for experimentation; and
- Develop intentionality to help children make discoveries and draw conclusions.

What Is Science?

Meet with the learner to develop an understanding of what is meant by science and what science provides for young children. Ask her to think about the factors that might need to be considered in setting up and conducting science activities. Ask her to give you examples of opportunities for science that she provides in her classroom. Use the following information to guide the discussion.

Science is:

- **Content:** A body of knowledge representing what we know about the world. Children have had limited experiences to draw on but have great curiosity and energy to explore.
- **Process:** A way of thinking and a way to discover the nature of things; activities related to learning about the world around us.

- **Attitudes and Dispositions:** A way of encouraging children to ask why and how. Reassuring children that their questions are valuable; fostering a sense of wonder.

Science is not just a collection of facts. Facts are, of course, a part of science, but science is much more. It includes the following skills of the scientific process:

- Observing what's happening;
- Predicting what *might* happen under certain conditions;
- Testing predictions under controlled conditions to explore if they are correct; and
- Trying to understand and make sense of our observations.

Science also involves trial and error—trying, failing, and trying again. Science does not provide all the answers. It requires us to be somewhat skeptical, so that our scientific conclusions can be modified or changed altogether as we make new discoveries and learn more. Science for young children is active, engaging, stimulating, and energetic.

Remember that young children are naturally curious, and in their pursuit of knowledge and to find out why, they experiment in many ways. Opening, poking, and shaking are all ways of finding out about something, and that's what science is. Science is a way of discovering and a way of coming to conclusions about the world and how it works.

Talk with the learner about observation—how we all learn by observing. However, discuss how children observe differently from the way adults do. Why is this so? Because adults' perspectives are different and our experiences are much greater. We have the knowledge built over years of experiences that allows us to interpret what we see.

What Does Science in Early Childhood Look Like?

Discuss with the learner the following information to guide her work in improving the science area for her classroom. Ask her to tell you other things she has noticed about how children approach science experiences.

Children have their own ideas. Children are natural scientists. They approach science freely and without hesitation and are not intimidated by the word *science*. From the time they were born, children have used all their senses to experience the people, things, and events in their lives. Remind the learner to keep this in mind as she sets up a science area. These experiences help children form their ideas, and their ideas often do not match current scientific interpretations. We should allow children to ask questions and make mistakes without feeling that they are wrong.

Hands-on works best. What engages very young children? Things they can see, touch, manipulate, and modify—situations that allow them to figure out what happens. In short, investigation engages them, and this is the very stuff of science. Hands-on science can also help children think critically and gain confidence in their own ability to solve problems. However, hands-on science can be messy and time consuming, so before you begin an activity, determine what is involved, including how long it will take.

Less is more. It's tempting to try to teach children a little about a lot of different subjects. While young children cannot possibly learn everything about science, they do need and will want to learn a lot about science. However, the best way to help them learn to think scientifically is to identify what they find interesting, to introduce them to just a few topics, and to explore these topics in depth.

Find the right activity for your class. Different children have different interests and, therefore, need different science projects. A sand-and-rock collection that was a big hit with a four-year-old girl may not be a big hit with a five-year-old boy.

Knowing the children in your class is the best way to find suitable activities. Here are some tips:

- Plan activities that are neither too hard nor too easy for the children in your class. If in doubt, err on the easy side because something too difficult may give the idea that science itself is too hard.
- Age suggestions on book jackets or toy containers may not reflect the interests or abilities of the children in your class. A child who is very interested in a subject can often handle material intended for an older group, while a child who is not interested in or has not been exposed to the subject may need to start with something recommended for a younger group.
- Consider a child's personality and social habits. Some projects are best done alone, while others are best done in a group; some require help, while others require little or no supervision. Solitary activities may bore some, while group projects may intimidate others.
- Allow the children in your class to help select the activities. If you do not know whether Sarah would rather collect shells or plant daffodils, ask her. When she picks something she wants to do, she will stick with it longer, learn more, and have a better time doing it.

Process Skills in Science

Discuss the handout **Process Skills in Science** on page 152 with the learner. Ask her to describe some examples from her classroom and to think about how she can begin supporting more process skills.

Photo Review

Show the learner some photos of science centers, which you have taken or you have cut out from school supply catalogs. Ask her to think about what is good about the setups and what features she would include in her own classroom. Help her assess what she has in her classroom already that could be used to set up the center, and ask her to evaluate the room arrangement to determine the best location for the center.

Finding What Is Needed

Use a school supply catalog to help the learner decide which items might improve her science center. Ask about items that parents might have on hand and be willing to provide, such as magnifying glasses. Help her make a wish list to prepare for purchasing.

Setting Up the Science Area

Discuss how the science area is not designed for all children to be in it at one time; its design allows for children to come and go. The science area should include only those items the children are free to use independently. Emphasize the free items from nature, such as leaves, twigs, rocks, pinecones, or seashells, that children enjoy exploring.

Brainstorm with the learner what the objectives might be in setting up or improving a science area. Use the following suggestions for ideas.

Science Center Objectives for Children

- To develop an awareness of the environment
- To understand basic concepts through exploration and experimentation
- To develop skills in identifying and solving problems
- To learn to formulate and test hypotheses and draw conclusions
- To use units of measure
- To develop classification skills
- To have opportunities to extend vocabulary
- To participate in proper handling and care of plants and animals
- To manipulate equipment and materials by engaging in various methods of discovery
- To discuss plans and shares ideas with others
- To develop positive attitudes toward living things, their interrelationships, and our environment

After determining the objectives for the science area, review with the learner the following guidelines in setting up a science area. Ask her how she might incorporate this information into her classroom.

Guidelines for Setting Up a Science Center

- Science can be a buffer area to separate noisy and quiet areas.
- Make sure the traffic pattern prevents interruptions.
- Clearly define the area using shelves or furniture.
- The science area can be composed of large tables, desks against a wall, a large windowsill, or even an area rug.
- If space is a problem for a permanent area, consider creating mobile centers made from trays, shoeboxes, or baskets that can be set out on a table as needed.
- Use the area to display collections, especially items from nature.
- Display materials at a height accessible by children so that they can see what choices are available.
- Separate materials that children can freely use from teachers' supplies.

- Make sure the area is visible from the rest of the room for ease of supervision.
- Make it inviting with attractive displays that will attract children.
- Encourage exploration.
- Allow children to add their own items to share with others.
- If possible, include an aquarium and plants to give children an opportunity to be responsible for caring.
- Provide materials that appeal to different senses: sight, smell, sound, touch, and taste.
- Change materials often to provide variety.

What Do I Put in the Science Area?

Ask the learner to think about what she should consider when selecting items for her science area. Point out that because science involves exploring materials and what can be done with them, there are some special considerations for selecting items for the science area. Use the **Guidelines for Selecting Science Materials** handout on page 153 to explore with the learner the items in her center or the items she plans to add to it.

Making a List and Checking It Twice

Discuss with the learner the following suggestions for science center materials. Ask her to create a list of what materials she has, what she wants to purchase, and what parents might provide.

Suggestions for Science Center Materials

A science area will appeal to children when it includes materials that encourage them to explore and freely use the materials. Materials in a science center might include the following:

- Ant farms
- Aquarium with fish, a turtle, or other animal
- Assortment of safe-to-use chemicals, such as vinegar, lemon juice, baking soda, and baking powder
- Balance scale
- Books about science topics
- Butterfly garden
- Classroom pets
- Color paddles
- Compass
- Feely box
- Flashlights
- Food scale
- Gears

- Hourglass
- Insect jar
- Items to sort and classify
- Items to take apart, such as a toaster (with plug and cord removed)
- Items with interesting textures
- Kaleidoscope
- Leaves, twigs, and pinecones
- Magnets
- Magnifier
- Measuring cups
- Microscope
- Objects from nature
- Pebbles

- Prism
- Pulleys
- Rocks
- Rulers
- Seashells
- Soil and seeds
- Tablespoons and teaspoons
- Tape measure
- Terrarium
- Timers
- Tuning fork
- Unbreakable mirrors
- Wire
- Wood

Picking a Concept to Be Explored

Show the learner a book or article about science activities. Ask her to select one activity for which she has all the necessary resources and that she feels would interest the children. Use the information below to help her plan and conduct the science activity.

- Select a concept to explore.
- Determine what she wants the children to learn.
- Select or create an activity.
- Decide if the activity is appropriate for the ages of the children in the room.
- Plan "messing around" time for learning.

The Adult's Role in the Science Area

Ask the learner to discuss with you what she views as her role in the science area. Use the information in the following list to guide the discussion. Point out that hands-on activities for children doesn't mean a hands-off approach for teachers; the teacher's role is very important in expanding children's knowledge and in supporting their questioning and experimentation.

The Teacher's Role in Science

- Prepare open-ended questions.
- Create a supportive, safe environment.
- Plan for exploration and experimentation.
- Encourage questions from children.
- Observe learning, assess children's knowledge, and expand on that knowledge.
- Help children look at things in new ways.
- Teach the language of science—use the correct terminology and watch how quickly children learn and love to use big, scientific words such as *viscosity, condensation,* or *photosynthesis.*

Discuss with the learner how the adult helps in the science area. Review the handout **Process Skills in Science** on page 152, and then use the following list of science process skills to work with the learner to identify how the activity she has planned can help the children in her class apply these processes.

- Observing
- Comparing
- Classifying
- Measuring
- Communicating
- Inferring
- Predicting
- Hypothesizing
- Defining and controlling a variable
- Exploring
- Understanding

Integrating Science into the Whole Curriculum

Review the idea that science can be a part of other areas of the curriculum—opportunities abound for teaching science in early childhood. Use the following information as a basis for discussing how to integrate science into the whole curriculum.

- **Art:** Fingerpainting helps children learn to perceive with their fingertips and demonstrates the concept of *color diffusion* as they clean their hands. Easel painting helps children see the effect of gravity on the liquid paint; it also helps them understand how the *viscosity* (thickness or thinness) of the paint affects how it works.
- **Sand and Water:** Concepts such as *volume* and *conservation* begin to be grasped when children measure with water and sand. *Buoyancy* can be explored with toy boats and sinking and floating objects. Seeing the differences between *wet* and *dry* sand and what can be done with sand in these two different states can be a learning experience.
- **Blocks:** Blocks are an excellent way to introduce children to *friction, gravity, balance,* and *simple machines.*
- **Library and Literacy:** Many books introduce scientific concepts while telling a story. Pictures give views of unfamiliar things and an opportunity to explore detail and infer and discuss.
- **Music and Rhythm:** These activities let children see how *sound* is made with air and to experience the *movement of air* against their bodies. *Air resistance* can be demonstrated by dancing with a scarf.
- **Outdoors:** The outdoors can provide an opportunity to observe *weather* and *changing seasons,* practice *balancing,* and experience *friction.*

Children will more likely retain concepts if these concepts are presented in a variety of ways over a period of time. For example, plan the following experiences about animals: a trip to zoo and a discussion of animals leading up to the trip, a study of animals, and learning different animal sounds. Expand the animal topic into the dramatic play area, the music that is available, and so on. For example, put animals' noses or costumes in the dramatic play area, and sing songs about animals. The connection between science and our world is stronger if children learn it in many different ways. Ask the learner to think of a science theme and use the chart below to plan how other interest areas can be used to expand on the theme.

Science Theme: Our Pets and How We Care for Them

Interest Center or Curriculum area	Activities	Materials and Supplies
Dramatic Play Area	Have a pretend veterinarian hospital	Stuffed animals, medical accessories such as smocks, white cloth bandages
Block Area	Children might build items for the animals	Rubber or wooden animals: dogs, cats, horses, or other possible pets
Music Area	Songs such as "BINGO"	Recordings and words to the songs selected
Library and Literacy Area	Books such as *The Pokey Little Puppy*, Clifford books; rhymes such as "The Three Little Kittens"	Puppets to act out the stories
Math Area	Children might sort stuffed animals by size	Stuffed pet animals in different sizes
The Community	Parents visit to show the class the family's pets; trip to veterinarian clinic or pet shop	Materials that reflect the children's experiences of parents visiting with pets or a field trip to a veterinarian clinic or pet shop

Science Themes

Seasons: Encourage children to bring items to the science center that they find in their environment. Make a special area of the science center represent the new season with pictures appropriate to the season.

Animals: Insects, birds, wild animals, farm animals, reptiles, and other animals are of great interest to children. Set up special interest centers on these themes, and encourage children to add items to these areas.

Measurement: Encourage children to bring in all kinds of measuring tools from home. Provide ample time for them to explore and manipulate the various measuring tools. Provide opportunities for free exploration with volume at the water table with pouring and filling various sizes and shapes of containers on their own. Other materials such as sand, coffee beans, and small pebbles or pea gravel can also be used.

Plants and Seeds: Provide many opportunities throughout the year to observe the growth of plants. The science center should contain plants for the children to care for. Seeds should be planted for the children to observe. They need to be actively involved in the planting process and in caring for the plants as they grow. The fall is a good time to begin seed collections. Children can be involved in the sorting and classifying of the seeds as they are brought into the classroom. Fall leaves are also a good source of material for sorting and classifying.

Science Activities

Discuss the following activities with the learner, and ask her to determine which science skills are supported by each.

Bubbles

Skills: naming and predicting shapes, identifying colors, understanding the concept of air movement

Use provided instruments to make bubbles. Have children make predictions about shapes that will be formed by certain items and identify colors formed by the sun's reflection off the bubbles. Have children predict the direction in which the bubbles will float and take notice of how the strength of air entering the bubble solution impacts the size and existence of a bubble.

Balloons

Skills: understanding the propellant force of air, predicting direction

Give each child a balloon. Before inflating the balloons, use a permanent marker to write the child's name on his or her balloon. The children inflate and release the balloon. They will recognize that the balloon is moving because of the air being forced out of the balloon by the elastic sides.

Safety Note: Closely supervise children as they explore balloons.

Putting It into Practice

Science Poster: Suggest that the learner make a poster to explain the benefits of science to the families in her class. Point out that such a poster will help families see the value of science. As a result, they may be more willing to supply items and to dress their children appropriately for the messes that science activities can sometimes create. The learner can also include this information in a parent newsletter.

Website Resources: Suggest that the learner begin a collection of good science websites to use with children. Help her to evaluate the websites and to store the information about the websites in an easily retrievable format.

Evaluation of Technical Assistance

Use the questions below as a worksheet or questionnaire to assess the learner's mastery of the technical assistance activities for science:

1. What are some important ways that science activities contribute to children's learning and development?
2. What are some guidelines for equipping and setting up a science area?
3. What is your understanding of the teacher's role in providing science experiences for children?
4. How can science learning be incorporated into other curriculum areas?
5. What are free or inexpensive items that can be used in science areas or activities?
6. How can you nurture children's curiosity and natural interest in science?
7. What are some objectives that you have for science learning for the children in your classroom?

Chapter 7 Technical Assistance:
Guidance and Classroom Management

What Is Guidance?

One of the most frequent requests for technical assistance is the topic of discipline. However, the request for help in the area of discipline actually represents a broader need to address classroom management. First, a classroom must provide interesting and challenging activities, a good staff/child ratio, and an appropriate schedule. Adult learners can use the technical assistance activities in this chapter to help them recognize how to help children develop self-control and discipline, through a classroom environment that is adequately equipped and staffed.

This chapter will provide experiences for the adult learner to:

- Understand what guidance is and what it is not;
- Learn to avoid problems by planning activities with consideration of the development of young children;
- Identify ways to communicate with children to get the desired behavior;
- Learn how to develop a cooperative classroom and how to set the classroom tone; and
- Identify specific techniques to address challenging behavior.

Guidance is helping children learn what behaviors are acceptable and what behaviors are not. Open a discussion with the learner about how she views guidance and discipline to find out more about how you may best help her. Ask the learner:

- What are your goals for the children in your class?
- What kind of people do you want them to become?
- Do you want them to behave out of fear or because they have learned self-discipline?

Why Is Guidance Important?

Discuss with the learner her ideas on why guidance and discipline are important. Help the learner understand that *discipline* is a quality of behavior that we want children to demonstrate, whereas *guidance* is how we teach children our expectations of appropriate behavior. The following are a few ideas that might be discussed:

- As early childhood professionals, we know there are positive ways to produce desired behavior.
- For children to develop self-discipline, we must teach them how to direct and control their own behavior.
- Guiding children's behavior is a process of building positive behaviors while reducing negative ones.
- Discipline is not strict compliance and obedience, but requires helping children to learn to control their own behavior and to see the value of that behavior.
- Guidance is not telling children what you *don't* want them to do; rather, it is showing children appropriate ways to do what you expect them to do.

Discuss with the learner how she views the terms and concepts of guidance and discipline. Below are some possibilities that might be suggested:

- Discipline is a quality of behavior we want children to demonstrate.
- Guidance is how we teach children our expectations of appropriate behavior.
- As early childhood professionals, we know there are positive ways to produce desired behavior.
- For children to develop self-discipline, we must teach them how to direct and control their own behavior.
- Guiding children's behavior is a process of building positive behaviors while reducing negative ones.
- Discipline is not strict compliance and obedience; it requires helping children to learn to control their own behavior—and to see the value of that behavior.
- Guidance is not telling children what you don't want them to do; it is showing children appropriate ways to do what you want them to do.

What Is the Adult's Role in Guidance?

Ask the learner to think about what she considers to be the adult's role in guiding children toward appropriate behavior. Discuss her beliefs and ideas about guidance and discipline and how those beliefs affect the children. Use the following list of possible ideas to facilitate the discussion:

- Children need adults to guide them and to help them learn acceptable behaviors.
- Adults can force children to behave out of fear, but in that process:
  - The child will only behave when someone is watching and becomes more concerned about being caught than the appropriateness of the actions.
  - The child's behavior is controlled from the outside rather than from within.
  - The child doesn't learn to value acceptable behavior for itself; therefore, self-discipline doesn't develop.
  - The child may see herself as a bad person or as unable to do what is expected.

- Instead, adults can guide children positively, teaching them differences between right and wrong, which results in:
  - The child learning to trust and care about others;
  - The child understanding the difference between acceptable and unacceptable behavior; and
  - The child developing the ability to correct his own mistakes.
- Parents want children to control themselves, and they want our help in knowing how to best achieve that goal.

Honest Answers

Ask the learner to answer the following questions. This task will help her to begin to think about ways to respond to children's behavior.

Think about This, and Answer Honestly!

1. In your opinion, why do children usually misbehave?
2. What are some appropriate actions you can take when children misbehave?
3. What behaviors of children do you feel could be better managed with more knowledge and understanding from you?
4. Are you able to accept and welcome change to enable you to better care for children?
5. Is there ever a power struggle between you and the children?
6. Do you realize that by offering choices, accepting children's developmental stages and processes, and maintaining your composure, you are still in control of a situation?
7. Do you work to prevent problems instead of punishing children once problems occur?
8. Are you willing to educate those outside the early care and education field who have different ideas about discipline?

What's the Best Way?

Ask the learner what she considers to be the best way to guide children to acceptable behavior. Lead her to understand that there is no one correct way for all circumstances; the best way depends on the child and the specific situation. Provide a copy of the handout **What's the Best Way?** on page 154, and use it as a basis for discussing some of the ways teachers can provide guidance.

How to Provide Guidance

Ask the learner to think about what she does now to provide guidance for the children in her classroom. If this includes punishment, discuss how proactive methods can help prevent her use of punishment. Discuss the limited effectiveness of punishment in changing behavior. Ask her to consider the list below and think about how she could incorporate some of these methods into her program. Use some examples you have observed to give her some practical ideas to try.

Guiding Children's Behavior

1. Help children learn to look for solutions and solve problems.
2. Guide children toward developing self-control and self-discipline.

3. Encourage children to be independent and gain confidence in their abilities.
4. Meet children's intellectual and emotional needs.
5. Establish clear expectations for children.
6. Organize the environment to prevent or reduce problems and support self-discipline.
7. Model respect and cooperative behavior.

Observation of Behavior-Management Techniques

Observe the learner interacting with the children. Note any examples of the following management techniques that you see her using:

- Modeling
- Reinforcement
- Planned ignoring
- Proximity control
- Direct appeal or logical consequences
- Redirection

After observing the learner, discuss the examples you saw and elaborate on why they were good techniques. Give her a copy of the **Behavior-Management Techniques** handout on page 155 for reference. Use the handout to discuss situations that she may encounter where one or more of these behavior-management techniques might be useful. Help her make a plan to try one of the techniques and to evaluate its effectiveness.

It's All about Prevention

Ask the learner to think about factors that indirectly influence how children behave. For example, crowding in the block area can increase conflicts; a schedule that doesn't meet children's needs can contribute to discipline issues.

Suggest that the learner focus on a child's behavior instead of on the child, saying, for example, "Thank you for putting your milk carton in the trash can, Annette," instead of "You're a good girl for cleaning up your place." Encourage the learner not to overestimate what young children are capable of doing or what the adults should expect from them. For good discipline, it is essential to know what young children are like and how to plan for them.

Ask the learner to consider her classroom and identify the changes she might make to improve the children's interactions, promote independence, and reduce discipline issues. Use the guidelines below to guide the discussion.

Providing an Environment that Encourages Self-Discipline

- Plan so children have few wait times.
- Remove temptations or dangerous objects.
- Anticipate dangerous situations.
- Keep the room well-organized.
- Store toys on low shelves.
- Help children learn to get along with each other.
- Plan the room arrangement carefully.
- Make use of symbols, labels, and reminders to provide guidance.
- Have the schedule posted and be sure it meets children's needs for movement, nourishment, and other physical needs, and is conducive to a balance of active and calm.
- Provide ample amounts of high-quality, safe toys.
- Offer a stimulating environment with much to see, hear, feel, smell, and taste in order to keep children interested and involved.
- Encourage the children to move around freely.

Using Positive Methods to Guide Each Child's Behavior

- Separate children who are hurting each other.
- Use the word *no* sparingly.
- Give children chances to make their own decisions.
- Use positive words to explain rules.
- Use facial features and vocal tones to express feelings.
- Try to understand why a child is crying.
- Work to understand reasons for a child's behavior.
- Let children say no to help them feel independent.
- Anticipate problem behaviors and act to prevent them.
- Make cleanup easy, and encourage children to do it.
- Give children many opportunities to explore and satisfy their curiosity.

Helping Children Understand and Express Their Feelings in Acceptable Ways

- Listen to children as they express their feelings.
- Work with parents and other staff to create plans to deal with challenging behavior.
- Model appropriate ways to express feelings.
- Encourage children to use their words to explain how they feel.

Guidance Strategies Focused on the Characteristics of Young Children

- **Adjust activities to accommodate for short attention spans.** Preschool children have very short attention spans. This means that they need activities to change often. They will not be able to stay in a group circle time for more than 15 to 20 minutes, and only then if the activities are changed frequently. For example, a circle time might include a story, a movement activity with music, a flannel board activity, a song, and another story. You might have five separate activities in no more than 20 minutes. The short attention spans of young children require you to plan many short activities for group time and allow many choices of activities during learning center times.

- **Avoid waiting time.** Young children do not wait well. Trying to get preschoolers to wait and watch while one child does a task is hard for them to do. Keep waiting time to a minimum, and when waiting is necessary, use the time for chanting nursery rhymes, singing songs, or doing movement activities.

- **Use small groups.** Young children function best in small groups. Allow most of the day to be in choice activities where the child chooses the interest area in which he wants to engage. When a child is offered different choices, he picks something he wants to do—which means he will enjoy it and stay with it longer. Children working together in small groups opens up opportunities for children to develop social skills, such as learning how to ask for turns, cooperating with others, and interacting respectfully with one another.

- **Recognize children's need for activity.** Young children are very active, so daily plans need to allow a lot of activity for this age group. Daily outdoor play is essential to give children the freedom to use large muscles for exercise and movement. Discipline problems may arise from trying to keep children still and quiet for extended periods of time. Plan for gross motor activity even on rainy days when the class cannot go outdoors. Substituting watching a video for outdoor play does not meet children's need for activity.

Dos and Don'ts of Guidance

Ask the learner to make a list of what she considers to be the dos and don'ts of guidance. The following are some possible responses she might give:

DOs of Guidance	DON'Ts of Guidance
Encourage	Yell
Praise	Threaten
Provide choices	Embarrass
Give nonverbal reminders	Shame
Communicate	Label
Use effective behavior management	Belittle
Have age appropriate expectations	Deny food
Understand room arrangement	Exaggerate the behavior
Plan interesting activities	Compare to others
Observe carefully	Use physical punishment
	Be negative yourself

Discipline or Punishment?

Talk with the learner about how people often equate the discipline of children with punishment. However, even though these terms are used interchangeably by some people, the meanings of *discipline* and *punishment* are actually very different. Use the information that follows to help the learner understand the difference and apply this understanding to her work with children.

Discipline or Punishment?

Discipline and *punishment* are the two words that describe what many adults do to make children "be good" or behave according to our expectations. Although children's behavior might be inappropriate for a certain time and place, children are not bad.

Discipline means guiding and directing children toward acceptable behavior. The most important goal of discipline is to help children gain inner controls. Teachers use discipline to guide children and help them learn the consequences of their actions. On the other hand, *punishment* means controlling children's behavior through fear. Punishment makes children behave in a certain way because they are afraid of what might happen to them if they don't. Punishment may stop children's negative behavior temporarily, but it doesn't help the children develop self-discipline.

The goal is for children to be able to control themselves. Why? So that they do not need an adult hovering over them to enforce every rule or to punish them for the least infraction. You probably have seen children who cower if you lift your arm to pick up something or who show fear when they have broken a rule. Then there are those who will not be honest about what they did because they are afraid of the punishment. The punishment that these children have received has not helped them develop healthy forms of self-control.

As professionals, teachers look at children's current and long-term development. The process of learning self-control is slow and gradual. Children need a lot of help, and some children need more than others. Helping children learn to control themselves takes a lot of time and a huge amount of patience, but it pays off greatly in the end. These children will grow to be responsible adults who feel good about themselves, who are trustworthy, who can make reasonable decisions, and who are a joy to know! When you teach self-control, you make an investment for the present as well as in children's futures.

Qualifications for Effective Guidance

Discuss with the learner the knowledge and skills needed to provide positive guidance. Have her finish the sentence that follows with the words that come to her mind. Some suggestions of possible answers are listed.

To provide effective guidance one must be:

- Knowledgeable about child development
- Knowledgeable about positive guidance techniques
- Understanding and know how to use active listening skills
- Know how to observe and record children's behavior
- Consistent

- Patient
- Respectful
- Responsive
- Sincere

Nonverbal Reinforcement of Desired Behavior

Ask the learner how she can acknowledge appropriate behavior nonverbally. For example, a smile signals "I like what you're doing" and a nod might indicate a yes. Ask her to make a list of other nonverbal reinforcements that she can try.

Using Gerunds as a Guidance Technique

Model for the learner the use of gerunds as a guidance technique. Gerunds are verbs that end with –ing, such as *walking* or *listening*. Gerunds are the shortest, simplest, and most gentle reminder for children; they get children's attention because they are short and direct. For example, simply saying *walking* in a calm voice when children are running inside will get their attention, and they will slow down. Saying *resting* in a calm voice will help them know it is time to settle down and prepare for nap time. Children interpret the statement to mean "right now" and appreciate the brevity of gerunds. Their shortness also seems to have a final connotation, and they are less apt to lead to attempts to circumvent the direction.

Point out how gerunds serve as a reminder of rules that children already know but may have forgotten at the moment as they are distracted by other interests or issues.

Use the activity **Gerunds** on page 156 to help the learner understand how to use gerunds. Ask her to try using gerunds in the following week and to report to you how it worked for her when you meet again.

What the Child Hears

Discuss with the learner how sometimes teachers say one thing but the child hears something different. Look at the examples below and ask the learner to give examples from her own classroom.

What Teachers Say	What the Child Hears and the Effect
"Would you like to come with me to the clay table? We can make vases together."	Redirection: There are other things to do.
"Just look at the mess you've made!"	Shame: I am a bad person.
"Tomorrow I can let you try to use the water table again."	Appropriate actions: I will get another chance.
"Shadonna may not use the art table anymore today. She did not do what I said."	Inflexibility: There is only one way to do things here.
"Some paint got onto the floor right here. I'll help you get a sponge to wipe it up."	Encouragement: Making mistakes is okay.

What Teachers Say	What the Child Hears and the Effect
"This is a big mess. I showed you just yesterday how to keep from spilling, and you did it anyway!"	Shame: Making mistakes is not okay.
"The water needs to stay in the water table. We don't want to splash our friends."	Setting boundaries: I know what to do.
"We had to close the block area because Jasmine would not use it properly."	Blame: It is all my fault.
"You are doing a careful job of pouring sand today!"	Encouragement: I'm learning how to do things.
"You simply can't seem to learn the rules for the water play area!"	Discouragement: I can't do this.
"You can use the cups to pour water into the funnel or the scoops to fill the cups. Pouring on the floor is not one of the choices."	Appropriate choices: Now I know what I can do.
"No more water play. You must play alone the rest of the morning!"	Punitive: I'm being punished because I did something wrong.

Anticipating Transitions

Ask the learner to think about transition times and discuss how transitions can be problematic. Ask the learner to identify how she can let children know that a transition is about to happen and why such notice is important. Explain that knowing that a change is coming gives children a chance to adjust to and prepare for the change. Give some examples such as how a child might finish her art project because she knows that she needs to go outdoors soon. Some suggestions for announcing a transition might be singing a song, clapping your hands, counting, flipping the lights, or a simple notice such as saying, "Five minutes 'til cleanup."

Building a Cooperative Classroom

Discuss with the learner the importance of considering all the children in the class when providing guidance. Point out that children need to learn certain behaviors so they can get along with each other and develop social skills. Discuss the following four traits and how to develop them in a classroom environment:

1. **Friendship:** association, conversation, belonging
2. **Compassion:** recognition and expression of emotions, problem solving
3. **Cooperation:** consideration of others, negotiation
4. **Kindness:** caretaking, gentleness, helping roles, generosity, protection, respect, encouragement

These traits are the foundation children need to learn so they can help create a cooperative classroom that is a community of caring learners. Use the following information to help the learner identify ways she can develop a cooperative classroom. Point out the ways that the room arrangement and other factors affect behavior.

Foundations of a Cooperative Classroom

Supportive Environment:

- Clearly defined learning centers
- Traffic patterns that prevent interruptions
- Limited visual or auditory stimulation
- A calming teacher voice
- Posted rules in words and pictures
- Large blocks of time for free play
- Support of children's independent behavior
- Limited excessive waiting times or sitting for long periods

Supportive Interactions:

- Nurturing adults
- Setting guidelines with appropriate consequences
- Building trust and a sense of safety
- Being a facilitator and not a dictator
- Allowing the children the opportunity to voice their opinions
- Modeling respect for the children
- Using your presence to remind children of the expectations
- Teaching children the words they need to use to be a part of a group or to ask for what they want

Supportive Materials:

- Enough materials for sharing in small groups
- Room arrangements that support cooperation and working in groups
- Plenty of time and materials for self-expression and creativity
- Neatly stored materials on shelves labeled with pictures and words
- No broken materials or materials with pieces missing (to prevent the frustration when children cannot finish a task)
- Enough to do so children are not forced to wait to be involved in activities

Supportive Activities:

- Cooperative games to reduce competition
- Role-playing to teach conflict resolution and compromise
- Helping roles such as selecting children to hold the door for the group, to pass around the snacks, or to help make a new child feel welcome

- Books and stories about children who are caring and helpful
- Modeling cooperation and communication to address differences
- Helping children see the value of cooperating

When Prevention Doesn't Work: Addressing Challenging Behavior

During your conversations with the learner about guidance, she will probably ask what she should do when a child presents challenging behavior in spite of prevention strategies. Use the following information as a guide for discussing with her how to address challenging behavior:

- Look for reasons for the child's behavior.
- Offer children acceptable choices.
- Focus on the child's behavior in a very specific way.
- Help children learn problem-solving skills.
- Help children understand the consequences of their behavior.
- Recognize that an effective guidance provider understands the need for:
  - Consistency
  - Honesty
  - Respect
  - Positive attitude
  - Patience
  - Warmth and responsiveness
  - Active listening

Resolving Conflict with Children: Helping Them Talk It Out Together

1. **Get together.** Bring together the children involved in a conflict.
   Point out how each child is feeling and then say, "Tell me what's happening," or "Sounds like there's a problem. May I help you?"

2. **Take turns talking and listening.** Give each child a chance to express what he or she wants. Clarify the problem and define it as a shared problem. Each child gets to express his or her feelings, and then is shown the problem from the other child's perspective.
   Restate each child's point of view. Say, "Sounds like (describe how each child is feeling)," or "Let's see if we understand the problem," (and then restate the problem as described by the children).

3. **What will help? Brainstorm ideas.** Ask, "What can we do so that you both get what you want?" At first it will be necessary to role-play possible solutions. As children use the process more and more, encourage them to use each other as resources. Children who are not involved directly in the conflict can help brainstorm solutions.

4. **Choose a plan.** Help the children think about and evaluate possible solutions.
   Say, "Okay, (child's name) came up with a plan. Is that okay for you?" If yes, then proceed with the implementation of the plan. If not, try more brainstorming and repeat the process.

5. **Try one idea. Did it work?** If it works, talk about how and why it worked with the children. If it does not work, go back to brainstorming and try another idea. Remember, if children are not vested in the process, let them go about their business, but be sure to come back to the process later that day. Say, "Oh, look! You worked it out together!" or, "It looks like it's just not working out. How else could we solve this?" (Go back to step 3).

Adapted from *Teaching Conflict Resolution Through Children's Literature* by William J. Kreidler (New York: Scholastic, 1994).

Interrupting and Redirecting Behaviors

Discuss with the learner that when children are interacting aggressively, when children are in conflict, or when children are not following classroom rules, she may need to interrupt and redirect the behavior. Use the following information to help the learner understand some of the ways to tell that problems may be developing.

When aggressive behavior is about to happen:

- Laughing stops, and voices become irritated or louder.
- The children start complaining or talking louder.
- The children's faces show fear, anger, or distress.
- The talk moves from interacting to menacing.

Point out to the learner the following ideas about how to go about interrupting and redirecting behavior when she identifies any of the signs that aggressive behavior or other problems are developing.

To interrupt or redirect:

- Give the children information and offer assistance.
- Use conflict-resolution strategies with the children.
- Break the problem into manageable steps.
- Offer a way for the children to take five.
- Facilitate rather than direct the process.

Putting It into Practice
What Would You Do?

Ask the learner to read each of the scenarios below, and then discuss them with her. Ask her to give an example of a gerund, positive statement, preventative measure, and/or behavior-management technique to show appropriate guidance. Point out how this type of activity will help her be prepared as instances occur during her work with the children.

- Melissa hits Caroline with a plastic shovel in the sandbox.
- Tristan keeps knocking over Morgan's tower of blocks.

- Felicia is going up the slide instead of down.
- Jacob bites another child during story time.
- Evan takes the ball away from Collin.
- A three-year-old sticks out her tongue at another child.
- A four-year-old uses an obscene word.
- A four-year-old is angry at another and yells "I'm gonna kill you!"
- A three-year-old grabs a toy away from another child.
- A three-year-old calls another a racially derogatory name.
- A four-year-old spits at another child.

Responding to Challenging Behavior

Ask the learner to identify a particular troubling behavior and to use the **Responding to Challenging Behavior** form on page 157 to make a plan for addressing the behavior. Ask her to include family members in her plan and to solicit their help with following through at home.

Review with the learner the staff manual regarding policies on guidance. Discuss what might need to be changed and what clarifications might be needed.

Marking Progress

Because much of guidance is rooted in how the environment is set up and arranged, take before-and-after pictures of the environment as changes are made. Ask the learner to describe her experience with the children in the new environment and how it improved guidance.

Developing Room Guidelines: Ask the learner to develop some general guidelines for behavior for her classroom. Have her consider a way she can use those guidelines in determining what to do about challenging behavior.

Keeping a Journal: Suggest that the learner keep a journal or log of the challenging behaviors and the positive behaviors for one week. Point out that such a record can help her analyze her efforts and the responses she is getting.

My Philosophy: Ask the learner to think about how she might describe her philosophy about discipline. Ask her to describe it in no more than four sentences, and advise her to make a poster or parent bulletin board that describes her philosophy.

What I've Learned: Ask the learner to provide a presentation of what she has learned about guidance at a staff meeting.

Educating Parents: Suggest that the learner find an article about discipline intended for parents that is appropriate for her children's families. Ask her to make copies of the article, and encourage her to share it with families to help them understand her approach to guiding behavior.

Evaluation of Technical Assistance

Use the questions below as a worksheet or questionnaire to assess the learner's mastery of the technical assistance on guidance and classroom management:

1. Why are discipline problems often a result of classroom management problems?
2. What is the adult's role in providing guidance for children?
3. What are some reasons why children might misbehave?
4. What might you do to prevent discipline issues?
5. How might you talk to young children to promote appropriate behavior?
6. What are gerunds and why do they seem to work well with children?
7. How might you encourage a cooperative classroom?
8. What are some strategies to address children's challenging behavior?

Chapter 8 Technical Assistance:
Building Positive Relationships with Families

Families Are a Priority!

Discuss with the learner that by building relationships with families and involving them in her program, she is opening the door for communication and working together for the benefit of the children. Relationships with parents are the keys to a successful program. Make it a priority, and all will benefit.

Evaluation of Relationships with Families

Discuss with the learner each of the following questions to assess how she interacts and communicates with families. You may want to ask her to record her responses.

Questions about Daily Interactions with Parents

1. How do you communicate with parents?
2. How can you improve or increase everyday communication?

In recognition of the many family configurations that exist today, the terms *parent* and *family* used throughout this chapter refer to the individuals who are fulfilling the role in a child's life that is commonly understood as a parent or family member. For example, a grandparent, aunt, or foster parent may fill the role of parent for some children. Close friends or extended family members may fill roles we commonly associate with immediate family.

To support the young children in her class, the learner will need to recognize the configuration and makeup of the families in her class, and use the words and terms that are inclusive of specific children and their families as a group. The important factor for the child is that the adult or adults who care for him in these roles are welcomed, accepted, and encouraged to participate as a partner in the child's care and education.

3. How do you enlist parent participation in your program?
4. What could you do to involve parents more fully?
5. What issues have come up where you and parents disagree? What techniques have you used to resolve them in a harmonious way?
6. How can you improve your ability to help parents and children say goodbye to each other?

Thinking about Relationships with Families

Ask the learner to write a list of five things she has done to build a good relationship with a specific family. After reviewing the list that she made, discuss the items on the list, and offer suggestions for other things she might do to build good relationships with families. Then, ask her to think of a parent with whom she feels she does not have a good relationship, and make a plan to improve the relationship with that parent. Offer suggestions, and set a timeline to check back with her to assess her efforts and progress. Ask her to share other positive or negative experiences or results she has had with parents.

Reasons for Working with Families

Brainstorm with the learner some of the reasons for working with families. Use the following list as a starting point to the discussion.

When interacting with children's families, remember to:

- Recognize that the children's primary caregivers are their parents, and respect the parents' wishes for their child.
- Appreciate that families are varied, and respect the family's cultural background.
- Understand the child, and work with the child's family for the good of the whole child.
- Keep the door to communication open.
- Provide consistency between home and school.
- Give parents confirmation that they are respected.
- Understand that parents often miss important "firsts" and therefore, they want to know about special firsts that occur, such as when a child has learned to tie his shoes or to recognize his name.
- Provide consistency in guidance.
- Communicate policies and procedures so families have a common understanding.
- Keep parents informed and knowledgeable about the program.

Talk with the learner about how she may spend more time with the children than the parents do. Discuss how parents may look to teachers for support in the task of child rearing. Parents may want the teacher's opinion if they have concerns about their child.

Communication Is Key

Ask the learner to summarize three issues that require communication with parents. Taking one issue at a time, ask her to write or tell what she might say to the parents to open the conversation. Then, have her think of how she can explain each problem briefly, in a positive manner, and write down what she will say. Have her think of three or four questions that she wants to ask the parent, and ask her to write those down as well. Then, have her think of and write down what she wants to happen as a result of the communication. Role-play this communication exercise with her to help her become more comfortable with talking to parents.

Communicating with Parents

Brainstorm with the learner some of the communication methods she currently uses with parents, and discuss some she may want to consider. Use the following list and chart to help her see additional ways to communicate with families.

- Send home activity ideas to reinforce topics learned at school.
- Provide books or a list of books to read to children at home.
- Send home special notes about what the child has accomplished.
- Make a point to be available at drop-off or pick-up time to talk to parents.
- Make periodic telephone calls to let parents know about their child's progress.
- Hold special events, such as a Grandparents' Day or Open House.

Make a Game of It!

Turn the information in the following chart into a crossword puzzle or a matching game. Give these games to the learner, and use them to discuss how to communicate with parents and other family members.

Ways to Communicate with Parents and Other Family Members

Communication Strategy	Definitions
Bulletin boards	A special place to put information where parents can see it when they arrive and depart
Children's work	Given to parents to show them examples of what their child has been doing
Conference	A formal meeting, usually scheduled ahead of time; often a time to review a child's progress or discuss concerns
E-mail messages	Electronic messages sent to parent via a computer network
Home visits	Meeting the parent at the child's home; often very effective, especially just before enrollment; this can be very time-consuming
Media announcements	Notices sent to the news media to get a message to many people at once, such as when a school must close because of weather, or as a means of recruiting
Newsletters (electronic or hard copy)	A regular report, generally one to four pages long, that tells what has been happening, what is coming up, and includes information such as reminders or articles of interest to parents

Ways to Communicate with Parents and Other Family Members

Communication Strategy	Definitions
Notes	Short messages to parents, usually telling them about something that happened during the day or telling them something about their child or what their child needs
Short, informal conversation	Conversation held individually with a parent, usually upon arrival or departure
Parent handbook	A publication that is given to parents at enrollment that tells them about the program and provides information about fees, holidays, and requirements
Parent letter	A one- to two-page letter written to inform parents about changes in policy, remind them of issues, tell them about an upcoming event, or tell them about special activities
Progress reports	A formal document that gives parents information about how their child is doing and what their child has learned; this is not to be confused with a report card
Resource library	A collection of materials, such as books or copies of articles, that may be checked out by parents to help them with parenting issues
Telephone call	A personal call made to discuss a specific issue with a parent
Electronic communication	Website posting, e-newsletters, blog, or any other electronic posting

Saying the Same Thing—In Different Ways

Review the following statements from hypothetical parent memos with the learner. Then, evaluate the negative aspects of the statements, and help the learner to recognize that the negative example tells only what was done wrong. It does not communicate the steps to remedy the problem. Although the information is correct, it sounds cold and negative. Brainstorm positive ways to phrase the communication that will address the issue but will be more upbeat and helpful.

Negative: Many families are not providing a change of clothing on a regular basis as is required in the parent agreement. Our policy requires that you provide a change of clothing so that your child has clean clothes if needed.

Positive: Reminder: We count on parents to provide a change of clothing, and we appreciate your cooperation to keep the supply of clothing from running out. Please check with your child's teacher to see if you need to replenish your child's clothing, and if you do, please send it as soon as possible.

Negative-to-Positive Activity

Working with the learner, review the following information about turning negative comments into positive comments. Help the learner identify reasons why positive comments would be better received. Ask her to rewrite positive versions for each negative statement. Discuss why and how she wrote what she did. Ask her to practice making positive statements so that the words are comfortable; this will help her to begin to form a habit of stating observations in positive ways. Help her to see how much more acceptable the positive approach is.

Negative to Positive: Change each of the following negative statements to appropriate responses or solutions for parents.

1. He's been crying all day long and won't be quiet.
2. She won't stop hitting the other kids.
3. I can't take my eyes off of him for one minute.
4. She spends all day long in time-out.
5. He's just so hyper; I don't know what to do with him.
6. She wets her cot every day.
7. He isn't talking well enough and the other children cannot understand him. We're going to have to keep him in this class and not move him up this year.
8. She just will not sit still in circle time.
9. I told her four times to put on her jacket, and she wouldn't do it.

Removing Communication Barriers

Ask the learner to identify what she feels are barriers to communication with families. Together, make a list of the barriers she identifies. Discuss times that she felt uneasy in a setting or felt reluctant to engage in conversations. After she has identified some barriers, discuss with the learner how she can remove or reduce communication barriers. Use the following information to guide the discussion.

- Remove the desk as a barrier to communication.
- Stick to the issue without blaming the parent or the child.
- Focus on finding a solution that is best for the child.
- Don't take sides; be respectful of each parent.
- Acknowledge and recognize the parent's ability to help.
- Create a relaxed environment.
- Have an orientation where curriculum, expectations, policies, and procedures are communicated.
- Educate parents on developmental stages of learning.
- Have policies in place to deal with common issues.
- Have empathy for parents, but stay objective.

Parent Posters

Work with the learner to develop a poster for a parent bulletin board about the value of play for children or another relevant topic. Include information that explains the importance and benefits of play for young children.

Talk with the learner about keeping the bulletin board simple but making it colorful to catch attention. Point out how busy families need the information to be brief and concise. Describe how bullets can be used to call attention to particular points in a poster. The following are some suggestions for content to include on a poster about the value of play:

Play helps children develop:

- Leadership and independence.
- Social skills and confidence.
- Decision-making skills.
- Vocabulary and language.

Displays as Parent-Education Tools

Help the learner brainstorm ways that children's items, such as art projects, can be displayed in the classroom to demonstrate to parents that what children do in the classroom is important. Ask the learner to write a parent letter describing ways that parents might display children's projects at home. For example, she might suggest using magnets on the refrigerator, making placemats by laminating artwork, using removable tacky mountings to hang children's artwork on the wall, or framing children's artwork with real frames or mat board.

Communication Strategies

Teachers often need to provide information to an individual parent. Discuss with the learner the following information as a guide for communicating with parents one-on-one. Print the information on a large index card for ready reference.

To support clear communication:

- Write a short summary statement of the information, using only a sentence or two that summarizes the main point that you want to communicate.
- Explain and clarify the situation. Refer to the circumstances that led up to the event by giving some background information.
- Describe what happened, being succinct and accurate.
- Explain why you think this might be important information for the parent.

Eliminating Jargon

Ask the learner what the word *jargon* means to her. Explain that jargon is terminology commonly used within a restricted group or career field that usually is not understood by persons outside that field.

Explain to the learner that the jargon used in the early childhood field may be confusing to parents. Help the learner identify some common jargon and write these phrases or words on an index card. Then think of other, more common or understandable words to describe the concepts to parents, and write the more common terms or phrases next to the jargon. Here are some examples of jargon to get started:

- Developmentally appropriate practices
- Child-centered
- Child-directed
- Gross motor skills and fine motor skills
- Manipulatives

Ask the learner to try to find one way during the next week to use the more common phrase and to listen for more examples of jargon. An additional benefit of this activity is that it will help reinforce the definitions of the words.

Challenging Conversations

Ask the learner about any difficult conversations she has had with parents or any that she needs to have. Use the following scenarios to discuss appropriate ways to address the situations. Ask the learner to describe how she would respond and why. Offer feedback to her responses.

Challenging Situations

1. Steve is four-and-a-half years old and still comes to school with a binky in his mouth. He keeps it in for the first hour or so in the morning and forgets about it the rest of the day. His mom hands it to him when she picks him up and brings him with it the next day. Mom says to you, "My sister says he's old enough to stop needing it, but he just always wants it. What should I do?"

2. Patrick's mom addresses you, the teacher, over the top of the four-year-old's head, "I can't do anything with Patrick. The little brat is becoming just as stubborn his father." She turns to her son and says, "Patrick, go on and put up your jacket. I need to talk to your teacher."

3. "He called me nasty words—I can't even mention them—yesterday at bedtime. I can't stand that kid's belligerence. What am I supposed to do? Anyway, I don't have time to talk now. Gotta get to work. They've got me taking these computer classes at night now, and it doesn't leave much time for anything. Hope you can straighten him out. See you at 5:30."

4. You tell parents when they enroll that you find it works best for the child if the parent hugs and kisses the child, says "Goodbye, I'll see you later," and then leaves. Latoya's mom always hangs around at least 15 minutes and makes several false starts before she finally goes. Latoya is usually upset and apprehensive about her mom's departure.

5. Billy's mom seldom comes into the center. She stops at the door, waits for Billy to go inside, then as soon as he gets interested in a toy, she leaves without saying goodbye. You have tried several ways to address the problem to no avail. You schedule a meeting with her and begin the conversation as follows: "I want to be sure that Billy is comfortable here, and I believe he may be anxious about being left in the morning. Would you help me make him feel more comfortable by . . . ?"

Questioning Techniques and Making Suggestions for Change

Use one of the hypothetical situations listed previously (in the Challenging Situations section), and ask the learner to prepare for a conference with the parent in the situation. They may want to use another situation that they want to discuss. Encourage the learner to use the following questioning techniques in the "conference." Have her role-play with you what she wants to discuss with the parent. Following the conference, evaluate the results.

Questioning Techniques

When you need information from a parent, it is helpful to prepare yourself using the following steps to help clarify your thoughts and communicate effectively:

1. Know exactly what you want to ask (for example, what are the child's eating preferences at home?).
2. Think about or write down how you want to ask the questions, or even practice asking the questions.
3. Think about, write down, or practice stating the reasons why you need the information.
4. Be ready to supply any additional information that is needed or requested.
5. Prepare yourself to listen carefully to the parent's responses.
6. Write how you will use the information, including how you will reassure the parent about confidentiality if the issue involves sensitive information.
7. Be prepared to listen actively and understand the parent's response.

Ask the learner to describe any instances where she has needed to suggest that a parent make a change in how they do certain things. Ask about any current changes that need to be made. Use the following information as a guide to review strategies for suggesting a change. Have her use the questions to develop a plan.

Suggesting a Change

When you suggest a change with a parent, you want to put forward an organized, concise idea that will be easily understood. Here are some suggestions for preparing and presenting suggestions to parents:

- Give a brief description of your suggestion for making the change.
- State the reasons why you are making the suggestion and why it is important.
- Explain what the child, the family, and the program will gain if your suggestion is followed.
- Listen carefully to the parent's point of view.
- Be prepared to provide more information or answer any questions the parent might ask.

Suggest that the learner write the suggestion she wants to make to a parent, including several reasons she feels the change is needed, and describe to the parents how the change will benefit the child, the parent, and the program. Discuss the learner's approach with her. Ask the learner to try this approach and report to you how it worked. Provide feedback to help her assess her efforts.

What Information Is Useful for Parents?

Help the learner identify information that she feels will help parents provide the best for their child. For example, if they know how their child is developing, it will help eliminate some of the misinterpretation and misunderstandings about what children should be able to do at specific ages.

The following are information topics that might be helpful to parents:

- The values of play and other activities for children
- The significance of hands-on activities
- Suggestions for guidance
- The types of play materials and experiences that are appropriate according to ages
- The importance of enhancing language development through books and stories
- Information about child development
- The value of helping a child learn the difference between fantasy and reality, yet still enjoy using his or her imagination
- The importance of developing strong social skills

Discuss what materials are available for educating parents in these topics. Emphasize how it helps a program when parents are informed about what children need and how experiences in group programs can help children learn. Point out how many conflicts between teachers and parents are often communication problems. Ask the learner to think about the best way to communicate based on the information they want to share. Clarify that although they may give the parent suggestions, the parents will decide what to do with the information.

Planning a Parent–Teacher Conference

Why Conferences Are Important

Ask the learner about her program policies related to formal parent conferences. If the program does not have routine parent conferences, discuss some of the benefits of holding regular conferences. Use the following benefits as a guide for the discussion.

Parent conferences are important because they:

1. Keep parents informed and enable them to be active partners in their child's education.
2. Provide an opportunity for open communication to better understand the child's needs.
3. Let the child and parent know you care.
4. Give the learner an opportunity to plan a united effort to address any discipline issues.
5. Solve problems through cooperation.

Discuss the process of holding a conference. Give the learner the **Guidelines for Parent–Teacher Conferences** handout on page 158 and discuss the rationale of each guideline. Ask the learner how parents might feel if these guidelines are not followed.

Plan a Conference

To get the most benefit from a parent conference, the learner needs to plan each conference carefully. Use the following steps to guide the conversation. Ask the learner to contribute any additional steps she might consider. In addition to the following information, provide a copy of the **Conference Planning Form** on page 159 to help her prepare for a conference. Ask the learner to hold at least one parent conference, and then ask her to meet with you to discuss it.

How to Plan a Parent–Teacher Conference

1. Send home a note to let the families know that a conference is desired. The note should include the following information:
   - Purpose of conference
   - Possible meeting dates and times
2. Decide what to talk about. Set one or two goals for the conference.
3. Prepare an agenda to include the following topics:
   - What is your (the caregiver's) general impression of the child?
   - How is the child progressing in each of the developmental areas?
   - Do you have any areas of concern?
   - What goals would you like for the child to achieve?
   - What suggestions do you have for achieving those goals?
4. Plan the questions you want to ask, the points you want to make, and the suggestions that you would like to offer.
5. Collect samples of the child's work or examples of behavior difficulties.
6. Prepare to describe what you have done to address any problems.
7. Schedule enough time. Parents sometimes need time to warm up.
8. Be prepared to explain the following:
   - Your classroom expectations
   - The schedule and how much time you devote to each activity
   - Lesson plans and activities
   - Developmental checklists and observations
   - Opportunities for parents to participate in your program

Preparing for Challenging Conferences

Discuss with the learner that it is sometimes necessary to address an issue that might be uncomfortable or even unpleasant. Introduce one of the following problem scenarios, and then ask the learner to select a course of action. Role-play how the issue might be addressed. Allow time for the learner to think about how she will handle the situation and what she will say. Help her think about the outcomes.

Problem Scenarios

1. Mom dresses her daughter in multiple layers of clothing, even on a pleasantly warm day. The child is never allowed to eat sweets, even on special occasions. Lately, Mom will not allow her child to paint for fear that she will get her clothes dirty. She doesn't like for her to go outdoors but tolerates it with urging from you.

2. Dad often finds fault with other people. He smiled as he pointed out the typo in your newsletter. He was furious when his daughter's shoe disappeared in the sandbox. He rarely says anything positive about his child's experiences and often refers to how much she enjoyed "that other center" she previously attended.

3. Mom volunteers so much that other parents think that she is a teacher. She plans field trips, bakes special treats, and often donates toys and supplies. She often spends time in the classroom helping with serving snacks or helping on the playground. She treats the teachers with respect, genuinely appreciates the care her son is receiving, and is so actively involved in all aspects of his education that he is becoming withdrawn when she is not present.

4. Mom becomes upset when you set boundaries and limits for her son. Sometimes his enthusiasm overflows into disruptive or aggressive behavior. Mom is so permissive that even when he is out of control, she insists that "boys will be boys" and does nothing to guide his behavior. She told you yesterday that she did not want to frustrate him.

5. As often happens, Mom had too much to do and could not attend the parent meeting last Thursday. On Friday, she had to leave quickly and forgot to take home Jarrod's favorite drawing of an alligator. Despite newsletters and personal conversations, Mom claims that she is unaware of the activities and events at the center. She complains that she is too busy to become involved, even if she knew what was going on.

6. Dad comes to major functions but otherwise keeps his distance. No matter how friendly you are, he shows little response. You know his son would benefit if Dad took more interest in the child's education and progress. You make sure that Dad gets all parent notices, notes, and newsletters, and often talk to him about activities at pick-up time. He just does not seem interested.

What Is the Best Course of Action?

Present the list of situations below, and ask the learner to select the best course of action for each situation. Some possible answers are listed following the list of situations.

1. You have noticed that Mary, a three-year-old, is slurring many of her words. What should you do to get help for Mary?

2. Tim arrived at school with a large bruise on his leg. When you ask what happened, he says "Daddy did it." What steps should you take?

3. You have a child in your classroom who is having a lot of behavior issues. What steps should you take to help both you and the child?

Possible responses may include the following:

1. Document which words cause difficulty and what you have done as a teacher in modeling proper pronunciation. Notify parents of your concern, and tactfully give parents the names of several places that might be able to help Mary. Document what steps parents take, any progress, and any services received.

2. Document and notify the director. Notify Child Protection Services and continue to document any suspected abuse.

3. Ask for a conference with the parent to explore options for addressing the behavior issues.

Involving Families in the Program

Family Involvement: How to Get It, How to Keep It

After discussions about parent involvement with the learner, brainstorm and review some of the issues surrounding family involvement using the questions that follow.

Family Involvement Questions

1. Why is family involvement important or not important?
2. What are some benefits and problems that can result from family involvement?
3. Is there a possibility of too much involvement?
4. What suggestions would you give to parents looking for a good school for their four- or five-year-old? What should they look for? What questions should they ask?
5. How might you involve families in your program?

Have the learner suggest ideas about how to involve families, and write them on an index card. After the suggestions are made, emphasize that you will help her discover other ways to involve families. Point out that any appropriate help leaves her time for other tasks, thus providing for a better program. Give some examples of how families might be involved to begin the conversation. Stress that even though parents may not have the special skills needed to work with groups of children, it is important to find a way to help parents feel a part of the program.

How to Involve Each Child's Family: Have the learner make a list of the children in the classroom. Then, work with her to list beside each child's name at least one way that child's family can be involved in the program. Help her select up to five of the ideas to implement, and ask her to let you know how the ideas work out at the next meeting.

Parent Interest Questionnaire

Help the learner to create or use a parent interest questionnaire that asks about hobbies or skills that parents would be willing to share with the program staff or with the children. Provide the **Parent Interest Questionnaire** on page 160 as a sample and any other samples of forms as resources. Help the learner select the questions that are relevant to the families in her program and to the tasks and resources that she needs. After the form is developed and distributed, work with her to compile the results and to make a plan to involve the parents in the program based on their identified interests.

Parent Visitation

Discuss the ideas of parent visitation with the learner. Sometimes, caregivers resist having parents visit or observe in the classroom. They sometimes feel that the children will misbehave, the visit will be disruptive, or the parent might gossip about the program. Discuss how to arrange for parent visitation and ways to make such visitations successful. Often, communicating simple guidelines with parents not only helps address the caregiver's concerns, but also helps make the parents feel welcome. Work with the learner to develop guidelines for parent observation in her classroom.

Handling Conflicts with Families

Sometimes you will have to make a difficult professional decision about what is in the child's best interests. Sometimes parents will ask you to do something that makes you uncomfortable.

Ask the learner to decide on a course of action for each of the following situations. Offer feedback, and if necessary, offer suggestions of additional ways to handle the situations.

Junk Food: "Why do you spend so much money on juice? Jeremy just loves sweet drinks at home. And some of it has extra vitamin C."

Last-Minute Overtime: "I have to work until 10 tonight. Could you just take Kristi home with you, and I can have my sister pick her up there around 8? "

Spanking: "Just spank him if he doesn't listen. Then when he gets home we'll make sure he has learned his lesson."

Discuss with the learner that when situations like these happen, she must always decide what to do based on what is best for the child. Ask the learner to write how she would respond to these dilemmas, considering that she wants to balance her concern for the child with respecting the parents' rights to make decisions regarding their child. Discuss the learner's plan for each situation.

Putting It into Practice

Children's Books about Families

Ask the learner to locate at least three children's books that have story lines about families who are involved in their children's classroom activities. Ask her to read and summarize the story of each, and plan a way that she might use the book to stimulate discussion about parents being involved in children's programs. For example, the learner might read a story about a firefighter who visits a school prior to arranging for a parent firefighter to visit, or she might read a book about a parent taking a child to school and staying to visit. If you have trouble locating a book, make up a story, or let the children tell stories and make books.

My Favorite Toys

Ask the learner to select at least five toys that are popular with the children in the class. Have her find pictures of the toys in a school supply catalog. Paste or glue the pictures on index cards, and discuss what children might learn by playing with the toys. Ask her to write the information on the back of each card and keep the cards handy as a reference for talking to parents. The card is not meant to be given to a parent; instead, it is created for the learner to be reminded of the information about what children learn from the toy. Ask the learner to report to you on your next visit on how the parents responded to the information.

Professionalism with Parents

Discuss with the learner her concept of professionalism. Ask about how professionalism affects the way early childhood staff are perceived by parents. Together, make a list of what it means to be a professional. Use the following list as a guide:

- Dress appropriately.
- Use professional language.
- Offer assistance and help parents get information to solve a problem.
- Be aware of the classroom appearance.
- Maintain honesty and respect.
- Stay nonjudgmental of families, respecting diversity and culture.
- Maintain confidentiality; share information only with appropriate persons who can help.
- Be tactful.
- Protect confidential records.
- Don't discuss matters in front of child or others.

Discuss the issue of confidentiality with the learner, and ask her to consider how she would feel if someone betrayed a confidence. Discuss how betraying a confidence can harm reputations, weaken relationships, or harm the children.

Evaluation of Technical Assistance

Use the questions below as a worksheet or questionnaire to assess the learner's mastery of the technical assistance provided about working with parents and families:

1. Why is it important to the child that teachers have a good relationship with his or her family?
2. What are some of the ways teachers can communicate with families?
3. How can you change a negative message to a positive one?
4. What are some jargon words that you have used that might have no meaning for parents?
5. How can you approach challenging discussions with parents? Think about questioning techniques and how to make suggestions for change.
6. How can you include diverse family concepts in the curriculum?
7. What are some guidelines for successful parent conferences?

Appendix
Forms, Charts, and Handouts

Action Plan for the _____ Area

What doesn't work?	How I can fix it?	What do I need?	Who can help me?	When can I get it done?	What will it cost?

Action Plan for the Block Area

What doesn't work?	How I can fix it?	What do I need?	Who can help me?	When can I get it done?	What will it cost?
Children throw the blocks and knock down towers, creating a lot of noise.	Analyze the arrangement to see if it stimulates involved play. Allow the children to help create simple guidelines for the block area. Make the block area larger to reduce crowding by getting a larger rug to increase the boundaries.	A checklist for analyzing the block area	My mentor and director	In one week. Three weeks if anything needs to be ordered.	About $20 for a larger rug, though possibly more if the analysis indicates more items are needed
Children will not pick up the blocks.	Make it easy for them to put things back by creating a better arrangement.	Some dishpans to store the small accessory items; Some self-adhesive paper to show where certain sizes and shapes should go	My mentor and my aide	Tomorrow. I can get the dishpans and paper tonight.	About $20

Formative Evaluation Report

Date of Visit(s): _____   Date of This Call: _____

Name of Center: _____   Telephone: _____

City: _____   Zip: _____

Rating of Assistance Provided

	Very Good	Good	Not Helpful
Review of an environmental rating scale, such as ECERS, or other evaluation instrument			
Provided professional development information			
Modeled the activity			
Assisted with room arrangement			
Item(s)/materials received			
State's quality rating system (if applicable)			
Resources(s) offered and discussed			

Equipment grants, accreditation, training, brochures and handouts, or other _____

_____

Questions about Visits

How did the visit help you? _____

_____

What information was the most useful? _____

_____

What is your biggest problem in running your center? _____

Training

Do you have questions about the training we offer or about registering for training? _____

_____

Do you have any suggestions for improving the training offered? _____

_____

Do you have any other comments or any information you'd like to share about the visits? _____

_____

Satisfaction Survey

Name of Individual _____

Technical Assistance Provided _____

Please help us assess and improve the technical assistance you received by completing the questions below. Check the box that best describes your experience.

	Poor	Fair	Good	Excellent
How satisfied were you with your interactions with the consultant who worked with you?				
How effectively did the consultant interact with other staff?				
To what extent did the consultant use your time well in meetings, telephone calls, or other interactions?				
How effective was the consultant in helping you resolve the problems or issues specifically identified for the project?				
To what extent did the consultant clarify your needs and the scope of this project?				
To what extent were your requests and requirements met?				
Were agreed-upon deadlines met?				
Please rate our service in each of the areas listed:				
Responsiveness to requests				
Instructor and training skills				
Ability to relate and understand needs				
Suggestions offered and resources provided				
Personal interactions with all staff				

Please use the scale to rate your overall satisfaction with the technical assistance provided at your site: _____

Please provide any additional comments on any aspect of the technical assistance project, the professional providing the technical assistance, or any other relevant information.

_____

_____

_____

Family Child Care Home Technical Assistance Report

Date: _____ Arrival Time: _____ Departure Time: _____

Announced visit ☐   Unannounced ☐

Name of Provider: _____ Telephone: _____

Street Address: _____

City: _____ Zip: _____

Directions to home:

Number of children present: _____ Ages: ____ ____ ____ ____ ____ ____ ____

Related to Provider? Put Y or N in blanks: ____ ____ ____ ____ ____ ____ ____

Summary of technical assistance provided:

☐   Reviewed registration requirements
☐   Reviewed emergency procedures
☐   Completed Family Child Care Environment Rating Scale (FCCERS)
☐   Provided training information
☐   Provider already on Food Program

List other information provided: (i.e., CPR, First Aid, Community Resources) _____
_____

Modeled activity as follows: _____
_____

Provider interests or needs: _____
_____

Recommendations for follow-up: _____
_____

Item(s) received by provider: _____
_____

Signature of Technical Assistance Provider _____

Signature of Participant _____

(The signatures verify that the visit was conducted as reported, arrival and departure times are accurate, and materials listed were received.)

Advantages to Learning Centers

1. Learning centers provide a concrete and practical approach to defining a curriculum. Once centers have been established, the curriculum can be maintained in spite of challenges, including staff turnover or absences. Learning centers provide a reference for developing, organizing, and classifying skills and helping children see the relationships between objects and materials.
2. Center-based learning conforms to what we know about how children learn. The learning-center approach supports the early childhood education goal of developing children's desire to learn and to continue learning.
3. A small, well-defined space encourages children to interact and talk together, thus allowing them to:
    - Make plans together, building language and social skills.
    - Work cooperatively, taking turns and helping one another.
    - Negotiate and solve problems together.
4. Children can choose their activities and materials, allowing them to:
    - Develop a sense of control and independence.
    - Pursue activities that interest them.
    - Be more focused as they play, therefore learning more and increasing their attention spans.
5. A variety of learning centers offers children:
    - Many ways to develop skills.
    - Choices in what they want to do.
    - Opportunities to develop multiple intelligences.
    - Chances to use their areas of strengths to learn.
    - Opportunities to explore and express themselves in creative ways.
6. Learning centers can offer materials that vary from simple to complex to address the different developmental needs of children.
7. Children can easily get the materials they need and return them when finished. This feature:
    - Promotes feelings of competence and responsibility; and
    - Reduces frustrating situations in which children have to wait for help to get what they want.
8. When activities and materials are readily available to children, teachers are free to spend more time interacting with the children.
9. Well-organized learning centers support teachers as well as children. Teachers spend less time in maintenance tasks and in resolving discipline issues.
10. A learning center–based curriculum requires teachers to assess each child's use of the environment continually and make decisions on how to enrich each learning center to continue to expand learning.
11. A well-planned environment frees teachers to observe how children use the materials and interact with their peers.
12. A learning center–based curriculum offers one of the best strategies for individualizing the program to meet the needs of individual children.

Indoor Environment Evaluation Log

Furnishings

Meet Children's Needs	Need Improvement	
		Furniture matches the sizes of the children using it.
		Furniture is sturdy and not in need of repair.
		Space includes soft areas like rugs, cushions, pillows, soft toys, or a rocking chair.
		Furniture is arranged in a clear, safe traffic pattern.
		Sturdy storage containers are used to keep toys separated and organized.
		Designated areas—such as labeled cubbies, hooks, and shelves—provide for personal storage.
		Areas are labeled with words and pictures so children can return materials to the correct spots.

Materials and Supplies

Meet Children's Needs	Need Improvement	
		Materials and equipment are safe and appropriate to the ages and developmental levels of the children using them.
		Children are able to choose from a variety of materials placed on low shelves.
		Children can make choices and avoid conflict.
		There are no materials or equipment that are broken or present safety hazards.
		Teachers' items are separated from those intended for children.

Interest Center Areas

Meet Children's Needs	Need Improvement	
		There is adequate play space in each interest center so children are not crowded.
		Teachers have easy visual supervision of centers.
		Children's creative efforts dominate classroom décor.
		Displays are child centered; materials are displayed at children's eye level.

Room Arrangement Checklist

Library (or Reading) Area

- [ ] In a quiet location away from noisy areas
- [ ] Not in a direct line of traffic
- [ ] Separated from the rest of the room by shelves, dividers, or other means designating boundaries
- [ ] Books stored on a rack, shelf, or other means of displaying books, preferably with covers showing
- [ ] Includes a table and chairs, rocker, or rug and pillows
- [ ] Room for two or three children
- [ ] Attractive, items neatly displayed
- [ ] Other: _____

Manipulatives Area

- [ ] Low shelves for materials where children can easily get what they want
- [ ] Attractive, uncluttered display with items sorted by type
- [ ] Shallow containers for small items
- [ ] Workspace nearby, such as a table and chairs or floor areas for using equipment
- [ ] Related items near each other (for example, pegs next to the pegboard)
- [ ] Other: _____

Dramatic Play Area

- [ ] Away from direct line of traffic and quiet areas
- [ ] Space for active play for three or four children
- [ ] Relevant and meaningful equipment
- [ ] Items easy for children to use and replace when finished
- [ ] Items based on current themes and children's interests
- [ ] Other: _____

Block Area

☐ Away from direct line of traffic and quiet areas

☐ Low-nap rug to define work area, reduce noise

☐ Space for group interaction and active play

☐ Low shelves for storage

☐ Blocks stacked by size and shape; large ones on the lowest shelves

☐ Accessories related to curriculum focus easily available (community helper figures, vehicles, and so on)

☐ Other: _____

Art Area

☐ Is near quiet or noisy areas and used as a buffer zone

☐ Is near sink or cleaning equipment

☐ Shelf for art supplies and hooks for smocks

☐ No items that cannot be used freely for art in the area

☐ Has easel

☐ Other: _____

Science Area

☐ Is near quiet or noisy work areas and used as a buffer zone

☐ Table for display and workspace

☐ Picture displays above table

☐ Space for experimentation and using materials

☐ Other: _____

Evaluating Interest Centers

Home Living and Dramatic Play Area

- ☐ Are the boundaries of the home living area well defined by dividers, shelves, or furniture?
- ☐ Is the area large enough to accommodate several children at one time?
- ☐ Is the area orderly when children arrive?
- ☐ Does the area include most of the following: stove, refrigerator, sink, table and chairs, dishes and pots, ironing board, broom, doll carriage, doll and clothes, and telephone?
- ☐ Is the equipment in good condition?
- ☐ Is the number of children allowed to use the area posted?
- ☐ Are the utensils arranged in a logical and convenient manner?
- ☐ Do the children know the uses of the items in the home living area?
- ☐ Are the children aware that they are responsible for cleaning up the area?
- ☐ Are the dolls and clothes kept clean?
- ☐ Are there doll clothes that can be managed by the younger children?
- ☐ Are there towels for drying dishes and bathing the dolls?
- ☐ Are there covers and pillows on the doll's bed?
- ☐ Have dress-up clothes been provided for boys as well as girls?
- ☐ Are there accessories, such as purses, wallets, hats, scarves, shoes, gloves, and jewelry?
- ☐ Do the children have convenient access to dress-up clothing?
- ☐ Are dress-up clothes shortened so they are safe to wear and length does not pose a hazard?
- ☐ Are dress-up clothes kept clean?
- ☐ Is dramatic play also available outdoors?
- ☐ Are materials varied to suggest new play ideas?

Block Area

- ☐ Is the block area in a location free from traffic?
- ☐ Are boundaries clear and visual distractions minimized?
- ☐ Is the area carpeted to reduce noise?
- ☐ Is the number of children who can use the area posted?
- ☐ Is there a generous supply of unit blocks?
- ☐ Are the blocks arranged on shelves in an orderly fashion conducive to constructive play?
- ☐ Is there space to leave constructions overnight?
- ☐ Are there boards, trucks, trains, animals and figures, and other props to enrich the block play?
- ☐ Are accessories arranged near the block area so that children have easy access to them?
- ☐ Are there large, hollow blocks and boards or cardboard blocks for building larger structures?

☐ Does the schedule allow for long periods of time for involvement?

☐ Are mathematical concepts developed throughout block play?

☐ Are the children encouraged to engage in construction activities after a story, field trip, or other experience?

☐ Are the adults overanxious because a block or building may fall?

☐ Are reference materials available, such as books and pictures about airports and other buildings, to clarify, extend, and integrate learning?

☐ Is there a camera to take pictures of block structures?

Manipulatives Area

☐ Are tables for quiet activities away from strenuous and noisy play?

☐ Are the puzzles and other materials complete?

☐ Do the containers make it easy for children to use and clean up materials?

☐ Are teacher-made items added frequently and materials rotated for variety?

☐ Are there opportunities to reinforce skills by using similar materials?

☐ Are materials available in graded sequence so the children develop skills gradually? For example, are there some simple puzzles for the younger children and more complicated ones for those who are more advanced?

Science Area

☐ Are the children exposed to many sensory experiences firsthand?

☐ Is exploration of objects made exciting and encouraged?

☐ Are cooking and food-preparation experiences provided frequently?

☐ Do cooking experiences promote good nutrition?

☐ Are children involved in nature experiences, such as planting seeds, caring for fish, and taking nature walks?

☐ Are field trips planned to expand the children's view of the world?

☐ Is there adequate preparation and follow-up for field trips?

☐ Are water and sand activities available regularly?

☐ Are the children encouraged to care for equipment?

☐ Does much of the equipment serve several uses rather than just one?

☐ Are materials changed regularly? Do they relate to a theme or unit?

☐ Do the children participate in cleanup?

☐ Are the children's experiences used as a basis for language development and literacy?

Music Area

☐ Is there a variety of musical experiences?

☐ Is music an integrated part of the program using recorded music, individual and group singing, instruments, creative movements, and dancing?

- [ ] Is there a good music player available?
- [ ] Does the supply of music include a variety for quiet listening and rhythmic activity, as well as songs to sing?
- [ ] Is there open space for the children to move about freely for creative movement?
- [ ] Are there musical instruments available for experimentation?
- [ ] Is the emphasis on enjoyment rather than performance?
- [ ] Is music used as a motivator for other tasks, such as cleanup and transitional time?

Art Area

- [ ] Is the easel ready and convenient to use each morning?
- [ ] Are the paints fresh and clean?
- [ ] Are there brushes in several sizes?
- [ ] Are there smocks or paint shirts to protect the children's clothing?
- [ ] Are the children free to explore the art media without expectations to make something?
- [ ] Does the area have new materials added regularly for variety?
- [ ] Are recycled materials used often?
- [ ] Are materials organized so the children are able to reach them and put them away themselves?
- [ ] Is the number of the children who can use the area posted?
- [ ] Is the emphasis on the process rather than product?

Library Area

- [ ] Is the library area attractive?
- [ ] Is the area carpeted and away from noisy interest areas?
- [ ] Is the number of children who can use the area posted?
- [ ] Are books correlated and rotated according to themes and children's interests?
- [ ] Are books in good condition and easily available for children?
- [ ] Is there a chair or floor area for a child to look at books comfortably?
- [ ] Are books displayed attractively on a shelf or laid open on the table to attract attention and invite interest?
- [ ] Is story time ever held outdoors?
- [ ] Do the children know how to handle books carefully?
- [ ] Do the children know to give torn or damaged books to the teacher for repairs?
- [ ] Are the children aware they are responsible for cleaning up the library area?
- [ ] Do favorite books remain on the shelves longer?

Suggestions to Build On

Home Living and Dramatic Play Area

- ☐ Child-size furniture, such as stove, refrigerator, tables, chairs, bed, and ironing board
- ☐ Dishes
- ☐ Pots and pans
- ☐ Cooking utensils
- ☐ Dress-up clothes, including shoes and hats
- ☐ Mirrors
- ☐ Books and magazines
- ☐ Telephones

Science Area (an area in which to participate, not just observe)

- ☐ Magnifying glass
- ☐ Animals
- ☐ Seeds
- ☐ Plants
- ☐ Touch, listening, and smell boxes
- ☐ Old clock and/or radio and tools
- ☐ Magnets and objects for them to attract
- ☐ Nests
- ☐ Water, funnels, measuring cups and spoons
- ☐ Cooking experiences
- ☐ Tools for weights and measures
- ☐ Balance scales

Block Area

- ☐ Unit blocks
- ☐ Smaller blocks
- ☐ Flat rug to cushion noise
- ☐ Trucks, cars, and other small wheeled toys
- ☐ Traffic signs
- ☐ Wooden, plastic, or rubber people and animals

Library and Listening Area

- ☐ 10–20 books, rotated and renewed regularly
- ☐ Rug
- ☐ Small table and chairs
- ☐ Bookshelves
- ☐ Stuffed animals
- ☐ Flannel board and flannel stories
- ☐ Puppet theater and puppets

Manipulatives Area

- ☐ Puzzles
- ☐ Lotto puzzles
- ☐ Construction toys
- ☐ Parquetry blocks
- ☐ Mosaics
- ☐ Number manipulatives
- ☐ Beads and laces for stringing
- ☐ Lacing cards
- ☐ Pegboards and pegs
- ☐ Table blocks
- ☐ Other materials that match shapes, sizes, colors and that allow the children the opportunity to use the materials in more than one way

Art Area

- ☐ Easels with clean paints and brushes
- ☐ Art table for art activities
- ☐ Modeling clay
- ☐ Glue
- ☐ Paper bags and boxes
- ☐ Collage materials
- ☐ Stitchery materials
- ☐ Sponges
- ☐ Chalk
- ☐ Assorted paper
- ☐ Crayons and markers
- ☐ Scissors
- ☐ String, straws, and other creative materials
- ☐ Art shelf with materials that the child may select at any time

Music Area

- ☐ Music player and recorder
- ☐ Headphones
- ☐ Musical instruments, such as bells, triangles, rhythm sticks, wood blocks, tambourines, maracas
- ☐ Props for movement, such as scarves and flowing cloths
- ☐ Space for movement

Sand and Water Area

- ☐ Sandboxes
- ☐ Water table
- ☐ Shovels, spoons
- ☐ Props, such as play people, houses, cars, and trees

Benefits of Free or Dramatic Play (Organized by Developmental Domain)

Creative

- Enjoyment of process
- Generation of new possibilities and ideas
- Use of the mental process of imagination
- Flexibility of thought
- Problem-solving skills
- Expression of personal uniqueness—self-expression
- Use of pretend and "as if" situations
- New uses of familiar equipment
- Creation of new roles

Emotional

- Clarification and better understanding of own feelings
- Ability to control own feelings
- Expression of feelings in a safe, nonretaliatory environment
- Feelings of delight and satisfaction
- Feelings of relief when anxieties are played through
- Feelings of freedom from adult standards and expectations
- Sense of mastery and control over what's happening
- Development of empathy; insight into how other people feel

Social

- Ability to get what the child wants peacefully
- Generation of skills related to entering a group
- Development of cooperative skills
- Grasp of social roles
- Differentiation between self and others
- Insight about other cultures

Physical

- Practice of emerging skills
- Use of small-muscle skills
- Use of large-muscle skills
- Coordination of subskills
- Attempts and successes at challenging new skills
- Experimenting and taking risks in a safe environment
- Integration of language with physical action

Cognitive

- Ability to extend and expand on ideas
- Use of symbols in place of real objects
- Development of advance plans and scenarios
- Clarification of information about the world
- Experimentation and drawing conclusions by trying things out
- Use of language to express ideas to others
- Use of signs and labels
- Ability to tell real from pretend

Setting Up a Dramatic Play Dress-Up Area

Gather an assortment of items that children can use for dress-up play. Make sure you provide items for the boys! Some suggestions:

- Dresses and skirts—no more than ankle length on children; cut off and hem if necessary
- Blouses and shirts—short-sleeve, front-button shirts are easiest for children to use
- Sturdy jewelry—no pins or small items
- Shoes—no high heels
- Aprons and scarves
- Purses and wallets
- Hats and gloves

Older children's clothing works well because it is large enough for young children to put on easily and small enough that it usually does not drag the floor. Ask friends and parents to donate items that you can use. Children's school-uniform shirts are good because they are often blue, beige, or white, which can represent uniforms of various types. Garage sales are also a good source of inexpensive, fun accessories. Wash in very hot water before use and as needed.

Initially, put a few choice items in a plastic laundry basket or other container to make it easy for children to select and return items. A dress-up area usually works best if placed near the home living area or in an area where there is plenty of room to move around and create play scenarios.

As children use the items and learn to use them appropriately, add more items so they have a better selection. If you see they are beginning to lose interest in the items or area, vary what is available. Replace items periodically when some are removed for laundering, and put in a few new items every few days.

The dress-up area can relate to themes that are a part of the curriculum:

- **Grocery Store**—aprons, purses, wallets, empty containers of food, toy cash register
- **Firefighter**—discarded vacuum cleaner hose or piece of water hose; man's or older child's blue shirt with "Fire Department" written on it; plastic fire hats
- **Post Office**—man's or older child's blue shirt with "U. S. Mail" written on it, large purse for mail pouch

Suggested Prop Boxes for Dramatic Play

Prop boxes are containers of related materials for use in dramatic play. They can be used as the basis for setting up an interest area or by themselves. To make prop boxes, secure and label boxes or sacks until you collect enough items for effective play themes. Transfer the items to a dishpan or a sturdy container when you are ready for the children to use them.

Young children re-create and integrate many of their experiences through fantasy and dramatic play. It is in this way children make sense out of their world. Teachers can help provide many opportunities for dramatic play by supplying the props and encouraging both boys and girls to assume a variety of roles. Chairs can become trains, cars, boats, or a house. A table covered with a blanket or bedspread becomes a cave or special hiding place. Cardboard cartons that children decorate can be houses, forts, or fire stations.

The following are some suggestions for prop boxes. Many of the items are free, inexpensive, easy to make, or readily available in an early childhood classroom. Use your imagination and see how many you can create.

- **Beauty parlor**—cotton balls, scarves, ribbons, bows, barrettes, capes (or aprons used as capes), plastic cosmetic containers, colored water in nail polish bottles, empty hair spray cans, wigs
- **Cleaning**—whisk brooms, sponges, towels or clean rags, spray bottles with water, small brooms, mops, cake of soap, sponges, toweling, plastic spray bottle, plastic basin, clothesline, clothespins, dolls' clothes to wash
- **Cooking**—pots, pans, eggbeaters, spatulas, spoons, plastic dishes, canisters, cookie cutters, disposable gloves
- **Dress-up**—sturdy jewelry (not pins), gloves, shoes, hats, purses, wallets, belts, scarves, ribbons (dress-up clothing will need a larger container)
- **Farmer**—child-safe shovel, rake, hoe, seeds
- **Florist or flower arranging**—various types of artificial flowers and greenery, plastic vases
- **Gardening**—gloves, toy rakes, plastic shovels, watering cans, plastic flowers, flowerpots
- **Gas station attendant**—shirt, hat, tire pump, tools, empty oil cans
- **House painter**—paintbrushes, buckets filled with water, white uniform with hat
- **Laundry**—clothesline, clothespins, doll clothes, handkerchiefs or small hand towels to wash, soap, toy iron, and ironing board
- **Mechanic**—assorted nuts and bolts, toy tools, plastic tool kit, tan or brown shirts with "Mechanic" written over the pocket
- **Medical (doctor or nurse)**—strips of white cloth, stethoscope, doctor and nurse hats, white shirt or smock, disposable gloves, shoe covers, adhesive bandages, cotton balls
- **Milkman**—plastic bottles and cartons, wagon, white hat and coat
- **Office**—toy telephone, old telephone book, toy or old typewriter, paper, crayons, envelopes, bank deposit slips, old calendars, calculators
- **Pet store**—pet carriers, stuffed animals, food dishes, toys for pets
- **Picnic**—paper bags, paper and plastic dishes, toy food or pictures of picnic foods mounted on cardboard, old tablecloths or sheets, basket
- **Plumber**—child-safe wrench, plastic pipes, child-safe tool kit

- **Police officer**—hat, badge, play cars and motorcycles
- **Post office**—toy mailbox (or one made from a shoebox), stamps (the kind you get in magazine promotions) crayons, paper, blue shirt, large purse (for mail sack), index card file, stamp pads, rubber stamps, pencils, old envelopes, box with sections to create mailboxes
- **Restaurant**—pots, pans, egg beaters, spoons, pitchers, salt and pepper shakers, tablecloths, aprons, notepads, pencils
- **Sand play**—plastic shovels, pails, transportation toys, flour sifters, funnels, items to use as molds
- **School**—chalk and small chalkboard, books, paper
- **Shoe shine**—soft cloths, small cans of clear (natural) polish, sponges, buffers,
- **Supermarket**—cash register, play money, paper pads, pencils or crayons, sacks, empty food containers, wax food, aprons.
- **Water play**—toy boats, empty plastic jars and bottles, spray bottles, funnels, corks.
- **Window washer**—bucket, soap, sponges, squeegee, water

Assembling Dramatic Play Prop Boxes

1. Designate a storage place for dramatic play prop boxes.
2. Collect a sturdy box for each kit to be assembled, preferably of the same type for ease with stacking and storing. A copying service or office might donate large boxes from cases of paper with lids; otherwise, purchase plastic ones.
3. Label the lid and end of each box with large letters for ease in locating.
4. Sort materials that you already have into appropriate boxes. This will get you started.
5. Make a list of needed materials that can be donated by parents or local businesses, along with an explanation of why you need the items. Involving staff, parents, and members of your community in assembling these boxes will prove to be rewarding for all.
6. Send the list home with the children. Post a list on the parent bulletin board, and cross out items when you get as many as you want. Request volunteers to contact local businesses for donations.
7. Request parental help for materials that need to be made, such as aprons and vests (vests can serve as flight attendant, conductor, police officer, or many other uniforms). Ask about outgrown, nonfrightening costumes such as dance costumes. Try local service organizations, such as the Girl Scouts, church groups, or senior citizen groups, for help in making simple placemats, tablecloths, or doll accessories.
8. Make a list of materials that will need to be purchased. Check thrift shops and garage sales for special items, such as galoshes for firefighters, containers for the beauty shop, and briefcases to use for luggage.
9. Fasten a list of items to the inside lid of each box so that the list can be used as a guide in returning materials to the right place.
10. Place the prop box where children can see what is inside before they use it so they will be less likely to dump everything out. Use a container large enough to make cleanup easy for children.
11. The materials themselves will usually stimulate play, but a story or field trip can also stimulate ideas. Therefore, they are excellent ways to introduce a new prop box. For example, your class might tour a fast-food restaurant to see behind the scenes what the employees do. You can bring back a variety of containers for your kit and set up a fast-food restaurant in your dramatic play area. Similarly, a trip to a fire station could add greatly to the play ideas with a firefighter prop box.

The Music Center

Learning centers offer children opportunities to explore their interests both individually and in small groups. In a music center, children can listen to music, play instruments, and experiment with sound independently and at their own developmental levels. Depending on how you set up a music center, you can also address multiple intelligences.

Consider the following as you set up your music center:

- **Location is critical.** Choose an area where children making noise will not disturb those involved in quieter activities. Try to find a spot near the dramatic play space or next to the circle time area. Remind the learner that she can designate certain times of the day when the music center is open or closed if noise is a concern. Also, the area should be large enough so children can actually move.
- **Make your center inviting.** Space, a table and chairs, and additional comfortable seating (throw pillows, scatter rugs) lets children know they're welcome to take their time in the center. Movement- and music-themed pictures hung on the walls will inspire the children and identify this as a special place.
- **Make the center accessible to young children.** Music players should be easy for children to reach and operate. Materials should be stored in easy-to-open containers and on low shelves to be readily available.
- **Change the materials periodically for maximum interest and experimentation.** When items are new to the area, the children will be attracted to them. Rotate items regularly to maintain interest in the music area.
- **Sometimes children enjoy dancing to the music.** When possible, allow space for physical movement.
- **Provide a music player designed for children and a wide variety of music.** In addition to commercial music intended for children, include some with recordings of the children's own voices.
- **Include a listening center with several headphones where children can listen to recordings they have enjoyed earlier.** If headphones are not available, the volume will need to be set low enough to prevent disturbing other areas and placed in a location away from quiet areas.
- **Include percussion instruments.** Choose maracas, tambourines, castanets, finger cymbals, and rhythm sticks.
- **Include a variety of sound sources.** Add paper bags or oatmeal containers filled with beads or sand, coffee-can or oatmeal-box drums, various sizes of stainless-steel mixing bowls, and wooden blocks or spoons.
- **Include melodic instruments.** Incorporate bells, small keyboards or pianos, tone bars, xylophones of various types, and, if possible, even a piano.
- **Add a prop box.** include scarves, streamers, elastic bracelets or anklets with bells sewn on, and rag dolls or stuffed animals to serve as dance partners. Collect items to supply several prop boxes so that the music props and available items are rotating. This helps to maintain interest and attract children to the area.
- **Include unbreakable mirrors.** Children can observe themselves and vary their movements.
- **Provide an ever-changing selection of books.** Children can look at while listening to music.

Making Musical Instruments

Tambourines

Materials: paper plates or pie plates, small jingle bells, string, hole punch

Allow children to decorate the plates. Punch five or more holes around the edges of the plates. Lace the strings with jingle bells between the holes. Tie and knot the strings together. Shake, shake, shake!

Maracas

Materials: empty water bottles, beads, superglue (teacher-only material), markers, tissue paper, streamers

Have the children cut the streamers and paper into strips. Place beans and strips in the bottle. Superglue the lid on. Decorate the outside of the bottle with permanent markers. Shake and enjoy!

Kazoos

Materials: paper towel rolls, rubber bands, markers, wax paper

Cut paper towel rolls in half to make shorter sections. Allow the children to decorate the paper towel rolls. Cut the wax paper in squares large enough to cover the ends of the rolls, with extra to hang over. Place the rubber band around the wax paper and end of each roll. Have children hum in the open ends of the rolls as they would in a kazoo.

Corn Shakers

Materials: dried corn (one ear per child), empty plastic bottle, glue

Give each child an ear of dried corn. Have the children pick the kernels off and place them in an empty plastic bottle. When the bottle is a third to a half full, place glue onto the inside of the lid and place the lid onto the bottle. When the glue is dry, the children have musical shaker bottles. This activity is also great for fine motor skills.

Finger Bells

Materials: gloves, jingle bells, needle and thread (adult use only)

Sew a bell on each finger and the thumb of each glove. The children put the gloves on and wiggle their fingers.

Hand Clappers

Materials: construction paper or poster board, scissors, crayons and markers, glue, frozen juice can lids, Popsicle sticks, tape

Have the children trace their hands on the paper or poster board and cut out the hand shapes. Then, let the children color or decorate them however they want. Next, glue a lid from a frozen juice can onto the backside of each hand that has been decorated. Tape the upper portions of two craft sticks to the backside of each hand. Once you have done all of this, take each hand, with the lid parts facing each other and the craft sticks coming out from the bottom, and put them together. Tape the two craft sticks together near the middle, more toward the bottom. When the children hold onto them and shake them, the "hands" will clap together!

Castanets

Materials: cardboard, large buttons, glue

Use a sturdy piece of cardboard sized about 1" × 5" and fold cardboard in half. Glue large buttons on the inside of cardboard ends. Click together to make a sound!

Cardboard Roll Shakers

Materials: empty paper towel roll (one per child), contact paper, rubber bands, rice or beans, wax paper, tissue paper, scissors

Place contact paper over one end of the paper towel roll. Secure with a rubber band. Fill it with rice or beans (you only need a small amount). Repeat on the other end. Cover the towel roll with tissue paper and tie together at one end. Then use scissors to cut the ends of the tissue paper in a decorative manner. Shake, shake, shake!

Outdoor Observation Form

Outdoor Observation
Observation Date: Time: Location:
Physical Skills
Language and Communication Skills
Mathematics
Science and Nature Concepts
Social Skills

Outdoor Safety Checklist

Layout	Yes	No
Is the space large enough to accommodate all the children in the group? Does it meet or exceed your state regulations? Quality standards?		
Is the space between pieces of equipment large enough so that children aren't running into each other or crowding?		
Is the slide or other metal equipment in a shaded area where it won't get too hot?		
Are drainage areas, electrical wires, and other hazardous equipment, such as concrete or hard anchoring material, covered?		
Are there no stagnant pools or puddles of water present?		
Is the area free of debris and obstacles or clutter?		
Are all riding paths clearly marked, gently curved, and separate from large-group areas?		
Is the playground fence in good shape?		
Are there both sun and shade areas?		
Is there a variety of age-appropriate equipment and materials adequate for the number of children who use the playground at a time?		
Are there areas for active and group play as well as for quiet and individual play?		
Are there clear pathways for children to follow so that traffic patterns do not conflict?		
Is the outdoor area defined so that children know where the play area begins and ends?		
Is there adequate protection from traffic or parking areas?		
Equipment	Yes	No
Is all the equipment solid and in good repair? There should be no rusted bolts, protruding nails, peeling paint, loose screws, loose connections, or splintered wood.		
Are all surfaces underneath play equipment covered with required or recommended impact-absorbing material, such as sand or wood chips, or with a manufactured energy-absorbing surface that extends as required or recommended on all sides of the equipment?		
Does the slide curve at the bottom to become parallel to the ground to prevent children's bumping on the ground?		
Are the slide handles, steps, and platforms in good repair and at the correct levels for the ages of the children using the slide? Are there protective railings? Is there an enclosed platform at the top adequate for children to get into position to slide?		

Equipment	Yes	No
Is all equipment appropriate for the size and development of the children who use the equipment?		
Is all playground equipment free of openings that might entrap a child's head?		
Is all equipment free of sharp points, corners, and edges? Free of rust?		
Are all tricycles and wheeled toys in good repair with screws tightened and handlebars secure? Are they the right size for the children?		
Is the sandbox clean and free of broken toys? Is it covered when not in use?		
Are water fountains and bathrooms easily accessible?		
Is there enough equipment and materials so that children don't have to wait for a place to play?		
Supervision	Yes	No
Do adults have unobstructed views of children at all times?		
Do adults move around and pay close attention to the children at all times?		
Are there established rules that children understand and follow (e.g., not to run in front of swings)?		
Are guidelines followed for required or recommended child/adult ratio when children are playing outdoors?		
Do the adults interact with children, talking to them about their activities and expanding on their observations, offering suggestions, and engaging in conversations about their activities?		

Note any improvements needed in the space below:

_____

_____

_____

Process Skills in Science

- **Observing:** using the senses to gather information. Observation is the ability to describe something using the five senses (sight, smell, sound, touch, taste). It is a fundamental skill upon which all other scientific skills are based. Strategies to reinforce observation skills require children to look carefully and watch closely for changes.
- **Comparing:** looking at similarities and differences in objects. As the children develop skills in observation, they will naturally begin to compare and contrast similarities and differences, the first step toward classifying.
- **Classifying:** grouping and sorting according to categories such as size, shape, color, and use. To group, children need to compare objects and develop subsets—for example, a jar of buttons to sort by color, size, or number of holes.
- **Measuring:** quantitative descriptions made by an observer. This can involve numbers, distances, time, or volume. For young children this might include two shakes of fish food, or a handful of sand. Measuring also involves comparing and ordering.
- **Communicating:** the skill of describing a phenomenon. A child communicates questions, ideas, and directions. Communication requires that information be collected, arranged, and presented in a way that others understand—for example, a weather chart in the classroom.
- **Inferring:** making meaning out of the observations. When one looks out the window and sees leaves moving, one infers the wind is blowing.
- **Predicting:** making reasonable guesses or estimations based on observations. A child may predict which of two plants will grow better: one that she waters, and the other that she does not water. When children observe, they wonder, guessing what something is or does. When they get an idea about what might happen, that is a prediction.
- **Hypothesizing:** formal conditional statements about what you are investigating.
- **Defining and Controlling Variables:** determining which variables in an investigation should be studied or should be controlled to conduct an experiment. For example, if a plant grows in the dark, will it also grow with light?
- **Exploring:** Opening the door, climbing into a box, and shaking a closed container are all methods of exploration or experimentation. The children are trying things out. They want to see what happens when they act on an object in a certain way.
- **Understanding:** Once children have worked with, played with, or tried out the object of their interest, they have some understanding of it. That was their intention, and they have been successful. This does not mean that the same child will understand all aspects or uses of that object, but he has gained some knowledge of it in this situation.

Remember: Young children are using science skills all the time as they observe, compare, measure, classify, and communicate about what they see happening around them.

Guidelines for Selecting Science Materials

- **Are the materials safe and sanitary?** For example, are the plants nontoxic? Are any of the items so small that they can be swallowed if children are very young? If activities involve food, are provisions made for separate spoons or individual serving dishes?

- **Are the materials open ended?** That is, can they be used in more than one way? For example, water play provides the opportunity to explore measuring or floating. Food-preparation activities involve many science concepts, such as heat effects, measuring, and senses.

- **Are the materials designed for handling and action?** In science, children do something to materials to make something else happen. For example, if substances are to be dissolved, which will offer the best experience: salt, sugar, or pudding mix? What happens when someone blows up a balloon? How is the sand different when it is wet?

- **Are the materials arranged to encourage communication among children?** If appropriate, place materials in such a way that creates cooperation and conversation. Arrange materials in categories, such as pitchers of water in one section of the center, substances to be tested in another, and spoons and dishes in another. Children quickly learn to cooperate and communicate in order to complete the activity.

- **Is there a variety of materials?** A wide variety of materials allows for individual needs to be met and for children to explore their personal interests.

- **Do the materials encourage "What if . . ." explorations?** A sink-and-float activity invites children to predict what will happen if they try to float various objects, such as a marble, a straw, a toy boat, or a sponge.

- **Are the materials appropriate for the maturity of the children?** Consider the maturity level of the children. Select materials that the children can handle safely and efficiently.

- **Do the materials allow for individual differences, such as ability, interest, working space, and style?** After considering floating and sinking, some children will begin to consider size and other characteristics of the available objects. Have available objects with a variety of textures and features.

- **How much direction do the materials require?** In giving directions, consider the age of the children. Four- and five-year-olds might receive directions from a recording, but three-year-olds and young four-year-olds respond best to personal directions. Rebus-type directions are also appropriate.

- **Do the materials stress process skills?** Process skills are the fundamental skills that are emphasized in science explorations with young children. These skills will come naturally from manipulating materials. However, a variety of appropriate materials is required for this to happen.

What's the Best Way?

Adults can use a variety of approaches to guide children's behavior. No single approach works for every child or every situation. The approach used should relate to the child and to the problem. Positive disciplinary approaches are based on the following beliefs:

1. The goal of guiding children's behavior is to help them develop self-discipline. Adults should guide behavior in ways that show respect and that help children feel good about themselves. "I'm going to help you up pick up the blocks so you can get ready to go outside. We'll find something else for you to do when we get back."

2. Very young children do not misbehave. They are not trying to annoy or control anyone when they cry or want to be held. "You are having a fussy day, Pam. Let me help you find a task that you will enjoy. Look, we've got new cookie cutters you can use with modeling clay."

3. There is usually a reason for children's behavior. Adults should try to find out why a child is crying or frustrated. "Maria's mother told me her puppy is not doing well, and Maria is having a hard time sleeping. Maybe that's why I find her crying and moody."

4. Children begin learning how it feels to have inner control by having some help from outside. "I am going to sit by you to help you stop throwing blocks."

5. Consequences should logically follow a child's actions. "Paul, I told you, you might hurt someone if you keep swinging that toy around. I'm going to put it away and help you find something else to do."

6. Children can learn from hearing positive language about which behaviors are acceptable. Use simple, clear language to help children understand you. Be sure that your facial expression and body language reflect what you are saying. "You may use the crayons on the paper, but not on your friend's paper unless he says it is OK."

7. Children's behavior is affected by the atmosphere in the room. Because children pick up on the feelings of their important adults, teachers need to figure out ways to support each other when they feel overwhelmed and tense. "Ms. Gonzalez, will you please help Frank? I need a breather."

How you guide a child's behavior depends in large part on the child's age and stage of development. In the first few years, children learn and develop very quickly. This guidance changes as they develop new skills, learn ways to communicate their needs, and become more skilled at controlling their behavior.

Behavior-Management Techniques

Note: None of these strategies will work if children are not given adequate activities and toys, as well as appropriate expectations.

- **Modeling:** Modeling occurs when a child learns by imitation. Children learn what to do and what not to do by watching those around them, including adults. Children are inclined to imitate the prosocial behaviors of a warm and responsive adult. When adults say one thing but do another, children may choose to follow the most lax standard of adult behavior. Be consistent, and practice what you preach! If you don't want children to sit on the tables, don't do it yourself, no matter how tempting.

- **Reinforcement:** Positive reinforcement consists of verbal and nonverbal rewards for desired behaviors. This reinforcement increases the likelihood that the desired behavior will occur again. However, be aware of what is being reinforced. Giving the child attention when she is misbehaving can actually reinforce the *undesirable* behavior. If we reinforce when they are behaving appropriately, they are more likely to repeat that desirable behavior. In other words, don't wait until they are misbehaving—catch them doing something right and reinforce that.

- **Planned Ignoring:** When a child engages in annoying but relatively harmless attention-seeking behavior, the best course of action is to simply ignore the behavior. The behavior often diminishes when it is ignored. The occurrence of the behavior may escalate when first ignored, but then, it will most likely decrease in frequency. While implementing a planned ignoring strategy, don't forget to praise and end the ignoring when the desired behavior is exhibited.

- **Proximity Control:** The mere presence or nearness of an adult can result in the discontinuation of unacceptable behaviors. Proximity control is usually very effective. The close proximity of an adult can have a calming effect on troubled children. Circulate around the room or playground, and your closeness will prevent many problems.

- **Direct Appeal and Logical Consequences:** Often a caregiver can quickly and effectively stop an unacceptable behavior through direct appeal to the child's sense of fairness. Caregivers sometimes neglect to simply and firmly state, "Stop this because . . ." When a child knows there is a direct consequence for misbehavior, the choice of how to behave is on the child. When misbehavior occurs, logical consequences should follow.

- **Redirection:** Inappropriate or undesirable behaviors can be stopped by distracting the child and engaging her in another activity without mention of the misbehavior. This technique can be very effective when children are quarreling over a toy or when a child becomes frustrated with a task or activity. Your interest in the new activity offered and in the child will make it appeal to the child.

Gerunds

Write the following statements as gerunds. The first one is done as an example.

Statement	Gerund
Please sit down and wait.	Sitting
Everyone is supposed to help clean up.	
Please pick up the toys from the floor.	
Everyone is supposed to be resting now.	
Jenny, don't bother Armando. He doesn't like it.	
When I said clean up, I meant right now.	
Sit in your chair without rocking.	
Please wait quietly while I get a book.	

For the next section, first rewrite the following statements in a positive form to tell a child what you want him to do, as has been done in the first example. Then, reword the statements as gerunds.

Negative Statement	Positive Statement	Gerund
Don't stand up when you slide.	Please sit down when you slide.	Sitting
Don't throw the sand.		
Don't jump off the ladder.		
Don't shout inside.		
Don't fight over the toys.		
Don't run when you are inside.		
Be quiet and listen to the story.		
Don't touch the cupcakes. They are for later.		

Responding to Challenging Behavior

Child _____ Age _____ Date _____

What challenging behavior is occurring?
How often does this behavior occur? How long has it been going on?
When does it happen? Is there any pattern?
How do you respond now?
How does the child respond?
Did something happen at home that might have upset the child?
Did something happen at the center that might have upset the child?
Conclusion:
Plans for responding to the behavior at home:
Plans for responding to the behavior at the center:
In about two weeks, what challenging behavior is occurring? Answer the following questions:
What happened at home or at the center when you tried your plans?
Has the challenging behavior changed or gone away?

Guidelines for Parent–Teacher Conferences

The teacher is the key to an effective parent–teacher conference. Use the following suggestions to ensure for an effective conference:

- **Be prepared**. Materials should be gathered and organized. Have portfolios, records, notes, and samples of the child's work readily available.
- **Provide a comfortable setting**. A parent who is not accustomed (as teachers of young children are) to the child-size chairs and tables may find them awkward. See that an adult chair is available. Avoid using a desk as a barrier. Let the parent sit beside you rather than on the other side of the desk.
- **Arrange for privacy and uninterrupted time**. To establish open communication, privacy and your full attention are essential.
- **Start on time**. Waiting can be stressful and can create unnecessary anxiety for the parent. Be considerate of the schedules of parents.
- **Greet parents warmly**. Call the parent by name. Conveying a sincere welcome and desire to meet with the parent can stimulate the type of rapport desired.
- **Open with positive comments**. Begin the dialogue with either a description of something thoughtful or creative the child has done or a significant achievement by the child. This approach shows the parent you see the good qualities in the child, and it helps build cooperation. Relaying an amusing anecdote or a kind, conscientious act can be effective in getting off to a good start.
- **Be approachable**. Be sure your expressions and body language are friendly and your attitude is optimistic. Maintain good eye contact with the parent.
- **Avoid jargon and esoteric terms**. Terms such as *perceptual-motor development* or *peer interaction* may not be in the parent's vocabulary. Be sure the language you use is understood by the parent.
- **Maintain two-way communication**. The purpose of a conference is mutual interaction. Do not do all the talking yourself. Open-ended questions or statements can encourage parental comments. "Tell me about. . . ." will generally produce more comments than "Does she . . . ?"

Provide information parents might need. Anticipate what might be helpful based on your recognition of areas of concern, and express a willingness to seek information concerning unanticipated needs.

Conference Planning Form

Child's Name: _____

Parent(s)/Guardian(s): _____

Scheduled Date: _____ Time: _____

Teacher: _____

Child's strengths: _____

_____

_____

_____

_____

Child's difficulties: _____

_____

_____

_____

_____

Suggestions for action at home: _____

_____

_____

_____

_____

Suggestions for action in the classroom: _____

_____

_____

_____

_____

Parent Interest Questionnaire

1. Are you interested in being regularly informed about the activities in your child's center?
   ☐ Yes   ☐ No

2. Are you interested in activities you and your child can do together at home?
   ☐ Yes   ☐ No

3. Are you interested in serving as a regular classroom volunteer?   ☐ Yes   ☐ No
   Weekly _____   Days you are available _____
   Bi-weekly _____   Hours you are available _____

4. Are you interested in visiting in your child's room?   ☐ Yes   ☐ No
   In the morning _____   At lunch time _____   In the afternoon _____

5. Can you provide refreshments for a holiday party?   ☐ Yes   ☐ No
   Which holiday _____

6. Are you interested in meeting other parents?   ☐ Yes   ☐ No
   If so, how often?   Monthly _____   Every other month _____   Other _____

7. Check the types of activities you would like to see included in the parent meetings:

   A. Social activities, such as
      _____ Potluck   _____ Family picnics

   B. Classes to learn skills, such as
      _____ Crocheting   _____ Sewing   _____ Photography
      _____ Computers   _____ Cooking   _____ Scrapbooking
      _____ Pottery
      List others: _____

   C. Classes to help with parenting or for general well-being as a family:
      _____ Family nutrition   _____ What to do when brothers
      _____ My family's health   and sisters quarrel and fight
      _____ Choosing toys and books   _____ Children's fears
                for children   _____ How to make games for
      _____ Discipline in the home   use in the home
      _____ Getting children to take   _____ Stress reduction
                responsibilities in the home
      Other: _____

   D. Information on community resources
      _____ Library   _____ Health services
      _____ Job preparation   _____ Social services
      _____ Recreation activities   _____ Cultural activities
      Other: _____

Index